BULLY PROOFING YOU

Improving Confidence And Personal Value From The Inside Out

BY JEANIE CISCO-METH

FORWARD WRITTEN BY
DAN CLARK CPAE

Printed and bound in the United States of America

The information in this book is designed to provide helpful information about bullying. Every reasonable effort has been made to ensure that the material in this book is accurate, true, complete, and appropriate at the time of writing. The information, strategies, and techniques contained herein may not be suitable for every person or situation. You should consult with a licensed professional where appropriate. The author and publisher shall not be liable for any omission or error or injury, damage, loss, or financial consequences arising from the use of the book. The decision of whether to use or not use the information, strategies, and techniques contained in this book is solely up to you.

ISBN: 0692481494
ISBN 13: 9780692481493

This book is dedicated to the people who are in pain because of the impact of bullies. May you hurt no more.

TESTIMONIALS FOR *BULLY PROOFING YOU*

"Bullying is everywhere. It's in our schools, our communities, our places of business, and even our sports teams. *Bully Proofing You* is the answer to this invasive problem. In this powerful book, Jeanie teaches you step by step an easy to understand format what you need to do to bully proof yourself for life. It is a must read if you would like be part of the solution and end bullying."
Dr. Jeffrey Magee, PDM CSP, CMC

//////////////////////////////////////

"As a step by step guide, this book contains everything you need to know. Brimming with straightforward strategies and steps anyone can use to over-come the key fears associated with bullying." Victoria Titova,
Author of *Miss Confident*

//////////////////////////////////////

"Anyone who's ever wanted to increase self-esteem, personal value and confidence will benefit from the down-to-earth knowledge in this book." Nicole Normand, Author of *Why Not You?*

//////////////////////////////////////

"If I could read only one book on bullying, *Bully Proofing You* is the one I would choose!" Adeline Heng, Author of *Doing Good and Doing Well*

//////////////////////////////////////

"A must-read for every parent and caregiver!"
Teo Chang Wee, Author of *Parenting 2.0*

//////////////////////////////////////

"Powerful, practical and solid advice on overcoming a lifetime of bullying. Apply Jeanie Cisco-Meth's knowledge and experience and step into your confident self once and for all!" Kenneth Low, Author of *Family Legacy*

//////////////////////////////////////

"*Bully Proofing You* cuts straight to the chase on what you need to do to make the most of the opportunities that come your way."
James Tong, Author of *Ignite*

///////////////////////////////////////

"Here is a powerhouse book of tips, tactics and approaches for *Bully Proofing You* that simply work. A fantastic book." Wendy Eng, Author of *Happy Free*

///////////////////////////////////////

"It's rare to find such honest advice on this subject. Congratulations Jeanie Cisco-Meth, I highly recommend *Bully Proofing You.*"
LENAghaz, Author of *Bye Bye Baggage*

///////////////////////////////////////

"What a fantastic, straightforward and honest book. A must read!"
Sheila Deb, Co-Author of *To Fight or Not To Fight*

///////////////////////////////////////

"So many people fail to overcome the effects of bullying. Jeanie Cisco-Meth outlines how to stop the cycle, overcome and succeed in life. A great read!"
Petronilla Muriuki Musau, Author of *Have Your Cake & Eat It Too*

///////////////////////////////////////

"Your inspiration and insight leaped from every page."
Lillian Miller

///////////////////////////////////////

"I read it cover to cover and it was inspirational and riveting."
Jan Conner

///////////////////////////////////////

TESTIMONIALS FOR JEANIE CISCO-METH

"Thank you for the support and positive influence you have been for Regan. I know you have helped him become better equipped to be a productive citizen and a good man." Alyson O'Steen, parent

//

"You did an outstanding job as a coach but even more so as a teacher..." Rick Majerus, Head Basketball Coach University of Utah

//

"I was totally engaged in Jeanie's presentation. She captured my interest from the beginning and held it for the total time. Great!" Franklin Deese, Mayor Marshville, NC

//

"Jeanie engaged the audience immediately which drew us in to her talk. She was very authentic and passionate about her topic. She touched my heart." Steven A Witges, Regional Vice-President, Farm Credit Services of Illinois

//

"*Wow*! That's all I have to say about your amazing class. You are one of those teachers students will remember forever." Jessica Allen, teacher

//

"Jeanie's easygoing personality makes her great to work with, and she has an extensive background that allows her to provide her clients with flexibility and variety." G. Brett Hart, ITT

//

"She constantly ties the lessons into everyday life." Lynn Gerratt, director, Alpine Summit Programs

//

"Jeanie, your book and class helped me realize I am worth more than I see myself as. I lived my whole life thinking I would never be anything more than I am and since reading your book and attending your class I see that I can be anything I want." Tawnie Orrilla McIntire, Student

////////////////////////////////

"Thank you for taking the time to come and speak…It's honestly opened my perspective on what life is truly about and on what my value means." Thomas, student

////////////////////////////////

"I learned how to stop bullies." Jace, student

////////////////////////////////

"Thank you for introducing me to a new world of learning." Gabby, student

////////////////////////////////

"The class changed my life." Lawson, student

////////////////////////////////

COMMENTS FROM BLIND SURVEYS

"She is one of the best teachers I have."

////////////////////////////////

"She cares about us a lot and wants to see us succeed."

////////////////////////////////

"I really think that she goes out of her way to be positive in every way possible every day."

////////////////////////////////

Foreword

As I read through the pages of this timely book, I was drawn back into my childhood memories of being bullied and the long-term, negative ramifications that those vicious comments and physical altercations can have on one's life. I am still scarred by those insecure souls who were stuck so deeply in their own self-pity and lack of ambition that they had to put others down to make themselves feel better about who they were. The only positive is the blatant reminder that when we lose our dreams, we die, and when we are not making progress, we beat others down physically, psychologically, and verbally so that we think we are.

The children then carry this resentment to school and act out to make themselves feel better about their low self-esteem, lack of self-respect, and need to feel dominant over those who are weak.

The good news is that this cycle of bullying can be stopped and replaced with awareness, education, and a step-by-step practical application plan for improvement. This is what Jeanie's book is about.

When you meet Jeanie for the first time, you notice her smile and then her height (and maybe even a cool hat). Her love for others and kind heart, combined with her knowledge and expertise concerning teaching, have allowed her to create a phenomenal book that will change the way we perceive and deal with bullies.

She writes like she teaches. She uses emotion to make the lessons stick and drive you to action. She knows that if she can get you emotional, she can get you in motion, and motion is the key to change.

Not only will this book give you the skills you need to bully proof yourself for life, but it will heighten your awareness of how prevalent bullying is in society, and galvanize your resolve to put an end to it in your school and in your neighborhood. Guaranteed that when you follow Jeanie's heartfelt message and her time-tested action steps, you will see immediate results and become an example whom others will follow.

Jeanie Cisco-Meth deeply understands why we all need to become bully proof, what we need to do right now, and how to do it. I strongly recommend *Bully Proofing You* to educators, parents, and especially students everywhere!

Dan Clark, CSP, CPAE
Author of *The Art Of Significance*
danclarkspeak.com

INTRODUCTION

Between stimulus and response, there is a space. In that space is our power to choose our response. In our response lies our growth and our freedom.
— *Viktor E. Frankl*

This book is for you. It is to help as many people as possible live rewarding lives. Everyone can overcome obstacles and become the people they want to be. Middle school and high school are difficult times. They are formative years that set you up for a life of learning and growing or oblivion and shrinkage. This time is when you learn to keep moving forward toward your goals, or let others take your dreams away. You can thrive, not just survive during your life.

When I was a young girl, I was different. People stuck labels on me when I entered school. I had so many learning disabilities and physical differences that I stood out. I had dyslexia, I couldn't speak well, I was legally blind, I was six feet tall by the eighth grade, I was a cancer survivor…the list goes on. Have you ever been labeled? How did it make you feel?

I remember sitting in the classroom with my parents, listening to the teachers predict my dismal future. I had different ideas. I knew I would find a way to succeed. I had a burning desire to prove everyone wrong and make something of myself. I knew deep inside that I could choose my destiny.

This book is all about the choices you make while you are in that space between stimulus and response. It is about how you shape your life with your beliefs and your reactions. I'm glad you decided to be part of the solution that is so desperately needed in our nation at this time. We can no longer allow the impact of bullying to take lives. There is an answer, and it is *Bully Proofing You*.

This book will take you through the steps to bully proof your life:

Step 1: Build your self-esteem so that you know you are a valuable person.

Step 2: Remember that it's about the bully's disappointing life, not yours.

Step 3: Learn how to ask questions that move people from survival mode to think mode.

Step 4: Practice in a safe environment.

You will learn the following from reading this book:

1. How to increase your self-esteem and personal value.
2. That you choose what you believe about yourself.
3. How to love and preserve yourself.
4. That bullying is about the bully's pain and hopelessness.
5. Why you should show the bully empathy.
6. That we are all connected and should respect life.
7. How to react appropriately when you are outside your comfort zone.
8. How to ask questions to stop a personal bullying attack.

9. How to stop another person from being bullied.
10. How to practice these skills in a controlled environment.

Many people helped me through school and impacted my life, but one person in particular stands out: Coach Pat Emerson. He was the Morton Jr.-Sr. High School's girls' basketball coach. He believed in me as a player and as a person. He thought I could be a great player if I worked hard and did my best. He instilled in me a determination to get better, to rise above where I was, and to make a change. He taught me the power of doing one more push up or sit up, adding more weight on the bar for squats, and pushing through the finish line while running. I learned from him that I was capable and tougher than I thought. He pushed me on the court and in the classroom. The best part was that he was always right there with my team, running one more set of lines or lifting weights. He never told us what to do—he always showed us how. He is a great example because standing in front of a group does not make you a leader any more than standing in your garage makes you a Porsche.

Thank you for taking a stand to stop bullying. Thank you for the time you are giving to the solution to this problem. Thank you for helping to create a better world to live in. Thank you for your willingness to grow. Thank you for being an example for others.

Jeanie Cisco-Meth

TABLE OF CONTENTS

"If I can dream it; I can achieve it"
—*Walt Disney*

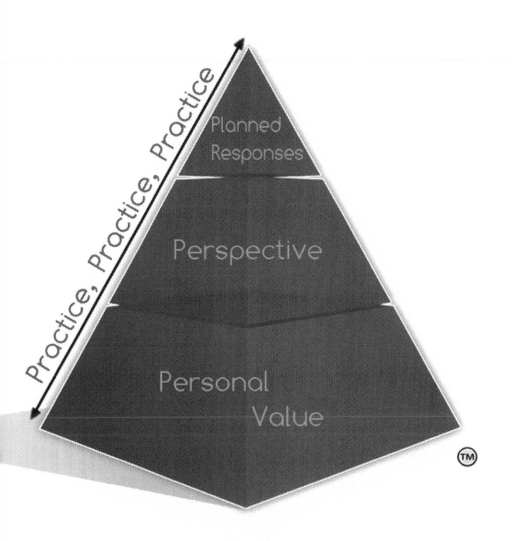

The Four Tiers of *Bully Proofing You*

SECTION ONE:
PERSONAL VALUE

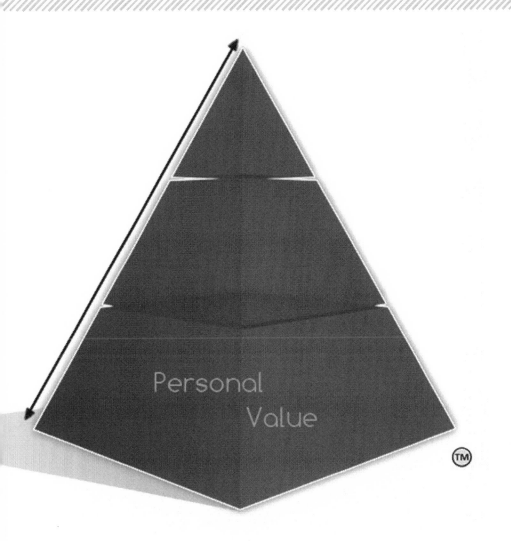

Dear Reader,

There is a workbook that goes along with this book. The more action you take to change the more likely that change will be permanent. You do not need the workbook to do the exercises laid out in this book. All you need is a writing utensil and something to write on but you must do the exercises. You need to get involved and take action to change. As you read this book it will have an impact on you; however, if you get involved and you practice, measure, monitor, and adjust you will change. You will evolve into a different person. You will change at a cellular level that will last your lifetime. You will be able to pass it on to others. That is my mission in writing this book. Change the world one community at a time by improving confidence and personal value.

You are now part of an elite group of people that are making a positive difference in this incredible world. I thank you for that.

If you would like to get my workbook, go to www.bullyproofingyou.com and contact me.

Thank you for your time,

Jeanie Cisco-Meth

I AM WORTHY

"You are worthy of all you desire because you make the decision, take action, and believe in yourself."
— *Jeanie Cisco-Meth*

You receive twenty-one chromosomes from your mother and twenty-one from your father. You come from these half cells. Nowhere but in the animal kingdom does this happen. Two half cells and a purpose created you, your family, and your friends. You have a purpose, a reason for living and being in this time, in this place. Have you found it yet? Do you know why you're here? If not, that's all right, because as you start to create your life, you will understand your purpose. You have a purpose.

Did you know that over 50 percent of pregnancies end in miscarriage and others in abortion? The sperm and egg that came together to create you were one in a million for the sperm and at least one in one hundred thousand for the egg. You are special just because of that, not to mention that you are the only one of your kind. In the entire world, throughout time, you are the only you. Even if you have an identical twin, you are still different. You are not identical in every way. You are unique.

Take a moment and look at yourself. You are no longer two half cells. You are a multisystemed, amazing being. You can do so much. Your brain is the most valuable computer ever made. There is nothing else like it. The electrical energy contained within you can power a city for over a week. The chemicals that make up your cells cannot be reproduced exactly. The value of *you* is priceless. While you are alive and thinking, there is no limit to what you can invent that will prosper this world.

You may wonder why this is important to know. You are worth the most when you are alive and thinking and living as you were created to. You add value to this planet. Could you imagine what our world would be like if Thomas Edison or Albert Einstein had played small and not done their parts? Think of all the people who have contributed to our comfort, entertainment, joy, livelihood, and wonder where we would be if they had not lived in their purposes. Still riding horses to visit Grandma? You are needed, so keep up the good work.

I mentioned purpose before and I want to expand on this. You have all the same parts that famous and notable people have. You just need to keep developing them. You can do anything someone else can do. In most cases, you can go further because you stand on the shoulders of giants. You can do things others have not been able to do because your knowledge starts where their knowledge ended. You can pick up what they learned and move on from there. You don't have to start from the beginning, so you can go further.

Imagine you have to run a marathon. Some people could do it right away. Some, like me, would need to train first, and some would never want to do it. But what if someone else would run the first twenty-six miles, and all you had to do was walk the last two tenths? Could you do it then? What if I told you that one million dollars would be waiting for you when you finished? Would you do it then? I bet you would find a way to make it happen.

That is what happens when you find your purpose in life. You will be focused like a laser, and a laser can cut through steel. Most people are like light bulbs that give off light but don't really go anywhere. When you are like a laser, you lead the way for others. Remember when I told you that if one person could do it, then you could also? You can be the example for others as well. You have done things no one else has. Make a list right now of at least one hundred things you have done, with no repetition. Go! (wb)

The first ten to fifteen were probably easy to list. Then it got more difficult. You might have gotten stuck and listed funny things. Then it got really deep and you listed the meaningful things, the things that make a difference in your life and in the lives of others. How does it feel to know that you have done all those things? For me, it felt like someone turned a high-powered laser on inside of me. It lit me up and got me going in a direction that has changed lives. Not only mine, but others as well. That is what you are meant to do, to find your purpose and make it happen.

I'm not saying it will be easy, because it won't. What I'm saying is that it is important. You were chosen to be here. A chosen one for this time. You must stop playing small and start making things happen.

Think of someone you admire. Now think what it would be like if that person had played small and not done the things you find amazing. What if that person had stepped back and said, "Oh, I can't do that. I'm not _____ enough." Your world would be different, and so would everyone else's. You also need to step up and find your path so you can make the world a better place. I don't know what you will do, but I know it will be great. I can feel it. I believe in you and your unlimited power. As Zig Ziglar used to say, "I'll see you at the top."

I want you to think for a moment about someone you would help if you could. Some people will immediately say, "I can't do that. Look at this long list of problems I have."

In my speaking engagements, I do an exercise with an orange to show people that no matter what kind of problems they have, they are still special.

It's the problems that make you stronger and better equipped to help others. You have skills from dealing with your scares that others might not have. You need to share your skills and strengths and stop hiding them out of fear. You might save a life, and it might be the life of someone you love.

One of my teachers shared this story with me:

One day when I was a freshman in high school, I saw a kid from my class walking home from school. His name was Kyle. It looked like he was carrying all of his books. I thought, "Why would anyone bring home all his books on a Friday? He must really be a nerd."

I had quite a weekend planned (parties and a football game with my friends tomorrow afternoon), so I shrugged my shoulders and went on.

As I was walking, I saw a bunch of kids running toward him. They ran at him, knocking all his books out of his arms, and tripping him so he landed in the dirt. His glasses went flying and landed in the grass about ten feet from him.

He looked up and I saw this terrible sadness in his eyes. My heart went out to him. So I jogged over to him as he crawled around looking for his glasses, and I saw a tear in his eye. As I handed him his glasses, I said, "Those guys are jerks. They really should get lives."

He looked at me and said, "Hey, thanks!" There was a big smile on his face. It was one of those smiles that showed real gratitude. I helped him pick up his books and asked him where he lived. As it turned out, he lived near me, so I asked him why I had never seen him before.

He said he had gone to private school before now. I would have never hung out with a private school kid before. We talked all the way home, and I carried some of his books. He turned out to be a pretty cool kid. I asked him if he wanted to play a little football with my friends.

He said yes. We hung out all weekend and the more I got to know Kyle, the more I liked him, and my friends thought the same of him. Monday morning came, and there was Kyle with the huge stack of books again. I stopped him and said, "Boy, you are gonna really build some serious muscles with this pile of books every day!"

He just laughed and handed me half the books. Over the next four years, Kyle and I became best friends. When we were seniors, we began to think about college. Kyle decided on Georgetown, and I was going to Duke. I knew we would always be friends, that the miles would never be a problem. He was going to be a doctor and I was going for business on a football scholarship.

Kyle was valedictorian of our class. I teased him all the time about being a nerd. He had to prepare a speech for graduation. I was so glad it wasn't me having to get up there and speak. On graduation day, I saw Kyle. He looked great. He was one of those guys who really found himself during high school. He filled out and actually looked good in glasses. He had more dates than I had, and all the girls loved him.

Boy, sometimes I was jealous! Today was one of those days.

But I could see that he was nervous about his speech. So I smacked him on the back and said, "Hey, big guy, you'll be great!"

He looked at me with one of those looks (the really grateful one) and smiled. "Thanks," he said.

When it was time for his speech, he cleared his throat and began. "Graduation is a time to thank those who helped you make it through those tough years. Your parents, your teachers, your siblings, maybe a coach…but mostly your friends… I am here to tell all of you that being a friend to someone is the best gift you can give them. I am going to tell you a story."

I looked at my friend in disbelief as he told of the first day we met. He had planned to kill himself over the weekend. He talked of how he had cleaned out his locker so his mom wouldn't have to do it later, and he was carrying his stuff home. He looked hard at me and gave me a little smile. "Thankfully, I was saved. My friend saved me from doing the unspeakable."

I heard the gasp go through the crowd as this handsome, popular boy told us all about his weakest moment. His mom and dad looked at me and smiled that same grateful smile. Not until that moment did I realize its depth.

Never underestimate the power of your actions. With one small gesture, you can change a person's life. There is no coincidence. God puts us all in each other's lives to impact one another in some way. You *do* make a difference. You impact others just by being in their lives. You may not know the effect you have at the moment, but you still have the impact. This next story happened to me in the early 1990s while I worked as a waitress in Salt Lake City, Utah.

I was a single parent to my beautiful daughter, Erin. Money was tight and we were on state assistance. I worked three jobs and attended the University of Utah. I knew that if I didn't go to school, our lives would be harder, and I had to go while she was young so she wouldn't remember the sacrifices. I am proud to say she never went to bed hungry. She always had food, shelter, and plenty of love.

Times were hard, and I didn't always know what was next. One evening while I was waitressing at Two Guys From Italy across from the Salt Palace where the Utah Jazz basketball team played, I had the privilege of waiting on Mark Eaton when he and his wife came for dinner after a game. People talked to him all evening. At the time, I didn't know he was a player for the Jazz. I just saw how nice he was to everyone who stopped by his table to speak with him. He never turned anyone away.

At closing time, my manager wanted to go home. I told him I would stay and let the couple finish eating because they hadn't had any time alone. I didn't mind; Erin was sleeping at Grandma's so it didn't matter what time I picked her up. Jose, the busboy, said he would stay as well. For the next few hours, it was just the four of us. I let Mark and his wife know the kitchen would be closing, but they could stay as long as they liked. I would keep their drinks full and serve them any dessert they wanted.

It was past two o'clock when they finally got up to leave. After Mark paid the bill, he gave Jose and me a one-hundred-dollar bill each. I was shocked. I had never seen that kind of money before, at least not in one bill! I didn't think I deserved it, but then Mark said, "You gave me a lovely, uninterrupted dinner with my wife. We don't get that very often and it means a great deal to me. Thank you."

As I drove home that evening, I thought about all the things I could buy: food, clothes, parts to fix my car. I had received a blessing, and to this day Mark Eaton is one of my heroes, and he doesn't even know it.

When you touch other people with positive energy, they are empowered to do things they did not believe possible. When I do an experiential training, I cut up a pen to show how we can take what we are handed and make a better "us" with it. You decide how others impact you. You decide who has power over you, and with that decision, you empower others.

I don't remember where the following story came from.

Many years ago, Al Capone virtually owned Chicago. Capone wasn't famous for anything heroic. He was notorious for enmeshing the windy city in everything from bootlegged booze and prostitution to murder.

Capone had a lawyer nicknamed "Easy Eddie." Eddie was Capone's lawyer for a good reason. He was good! In fact, Eddie's skill at legal maneuvering kept Big Al out of jail for a long time.

To show his appreciation, Capone paid him well. Not only was the money big, but Eddie also got special dividends. For instance, he and his family occupied a fenced-in mansion with live-in help and all the conveniences of the day. The estate was so large that it filled an entire Chicago city block. Eddie lived the high life of the Chicago mob and gave little consideration to the atrocities that went on around him.

Eddie did have one soft spot, however. He had a son whom he loved dearly. Eddie saw to it that his young son had clothes, cars, and a good education. Nothing was withheld. Price was no object. And despite his involvement with organized crime, Eddie even tried to teach his son right from wrong. He wanted his son to be a better man than he was. Yet with all his wealth and influence, there were two things he couldn't give his son: he couldn't pass on a good name or a good example.

One day, Easy Eddie reached a difficult decision. He wanted to rectify the wrongs he had done. He told the authorities the truth about Al "Scarface" Capone, cleaned up his tarnished name, and offered his son some semblance of integrity. To do this, he would have to testify against the mob, and he knew that the cost would be great. So he testified.

Within the year, Easy Eddie's life ended in a blaze of gunfire on a lonely Chicago street. But in his eyes, he had given his son the greatest gift he had to offer, at the greatest price he could ever pay. Police removed from his pockets a rosary, a crucifix, a religious medallion, and a poem clipped from a magazine.

The poem read:

> The clock of life is wound but once,
> And no man has the power to tell
> Just when the hands will stop
> At late or early hour.
> Now is the only time you own.
> Live, love, toil with a will.
> Place no faith in time.
> For the clock may soon be still.

STORY NUMBER TWO:

World War II produced many heroes. One such man was Lieutenant Commander Butch O'Hare. He was a fighter pilot assigned to the aircraft carrier Lexington in the South Pacific.

One day his entire squadron was sent on a mission. After he was airborne, he realized that someone had forgotten to top off his fuel tank. He would not have enough fuel to complete his mission and get back to his ship. His flight leader told him to return to the carrier. Reluctantly, he dropped out of formation and headed back to the fleet.

As he returned to the mother ship, he saw something that turned his blood cold: a squadron of Japanese aircraft speeding its way toward the American fleet. The American fighters were gone on a sortie, and the fleet was all but defenseless. He couldn't reach his squadron and bring them back in time to save the fleet. Nor could he warn the fleet of the approaching danger. There was only one thing to do. He had to somehow divert them from the fleet.

Laying aside all thoughts of personal safety, he dove into the formation of Japanese planes. Wing-mounted fifty calibers blazed as he charged in, attacking one surprised enemy plane and then another. Butch wove in and out of the now-broken formation and fired at as many planes as possible until all his ammunition was finally spent.

Undaunted, he continued the assault. He dove at the planes, trying to clip a wing or tail in hopes of damaging as many enemy planes as possible and rendering them unfit to fly. Finally, the exasperated Japanese squadron took off in another direction. Deeply relieved, Butch O'Hare and his tattered fighter limped back to the carrier.

Upon arrival, he reported in and related the event surrounding his return. The film from the gun-camera mounted on his plane told the tale. It showed the extent of Butch's daring attempt to protect his fleet. He had, in fact, destroyed five enemy aircraft. This took place on February 20, 1942, and, for that action, Butch became the navy's first ace of WWII and the first naval aviator to win the Congressional Medal of Honor.

A year later, Butch was killed in aerial combat at the age of twenty-nine. His hometown would not allow the memory of this WWII hero to fade, and today, O'Hare Airport in Chicago is named in tribute of the courage of this great man.

The next time you find yourself at O'Hare International, give some thought to visiting Butch's memorial display of his statue and his Medal of Honor. It's located between terminals one and two.

So what do these two stories have to do with each other?

Butch O'Hare was "Easy Eddie's" son.

Butch O'Hare decided to become a great man, like his father did at the end of his life. There are examples all around us of positive and negative influences. You decide which ones to listen to and believe in. Walt Disney said, "If I can believe it, I can achieve it."

You have to decide that you are valuable. You must believe that you are worthy of all that is given you, that you can do whatever you desire. It all starts with belief in yourself. Whether you think you can, or you can't, you're right. It's time to stop listening to all the negatives and tune into all the positives that come your way.

Find gratitude in the many gifts you have been given. Make a list of a minimum of one hundred things you are grateful for, without repeating any items. Do it now. (wb)

How do you feel? Pretty good, yes? When you place yourself in a feeling of gratitude, the world is a better place.

I challenge you to do this for the next forty days. (wb) Start each day with a grateful and glad heart. Your life will be fuller and richer. Opportunities will come to you that you hadn't noticed before. Use the words "please" and "thank you," as they show respect for others and for yourself. Start acting on the things you know will lead you to where you want to go. You'll be amazed at how your life will change.

To recap what you have learned in this chapter, I want to list the lessons here:

You are a high-functioning, created being with a purpose.

You must live your purpose so others can live theirs.

You are loved and cherished, and you matter.

You make a difference.

You impact others with your words and deeds.

You are worthy of your desires.

You need to be grateful for what you have.

You grow by taking action.

You show respect for others by saying please and thank you.

You can live the life you desire.

What you want to remember:

2

I CHOOSE WHAT I BELIEVE

"They themselves are the maker of themselves."
— *James Allen*

Think about the things you believe. You came to believe them because you agreed with the person or source the belief came from. That's all. If you didn't agree with the source, then you rejected what was said.

There was a time when everyone thought the earth rotated around the sun. Then Copernicus found out differently through study and observation. People believed that running a four-minute mile would cause the human body to fall apart. Then Roger Banister believed something new. He believed he could do it, and so he did. Within the next few months, three more people had broken the four minute mile. It's all about what you believe and how you act on that belief.

The wonderful thing is that you can change your belief when you decide what your new belief will be. The age-old hobby of blaming someone else for your beliefs is gone. You made the choice to believe what you were told.

Did you check to see if the beliefs were true or not? Now you need to decide if those beliefs still support you and your future.

Our beliefs lead to our feelings, and our feelings lead to our actions. Our actions lead to our habits, our habits lead to our lifestyles, and our lifestyles lead to our destinies. It all starts with our beliefs. Think about what you believe about yourself, the world, other people, opportunities, money, politicians, your parents, etc. When you question your beliefs, you open the door to new possibilities. You examine where you are and where you are going. If you never question or check in with your feelings and habits, you are on autopilot and you may not be going where you want to go.

When you are run by habits, you no longer control your trajectory. Your habits do. When I first heard the saying that you create your habits and then your habits create you, I didn't know what it meant. After I pondered it and rolled it around in my consciousness, I understood. If I do something for a while, then I no longer think about it. I just continue doing it. For example, most of us are in the habit of brushing our teeth every day, twice a day. We reap the rewards of no cavities. If we forget to brush once in a while, we might need some fillings, depending on our teeth and whether we had fluoride growing up. However, if you don't brush your teeth, you will have cavities and crowns, and maybe even need false teeth. Brushing your teeth is a little thing, or so it seems, but this habit affects your health. You don't get cavities overnight. You don't have pain the first time you skip brushing your teeth. You can go for some time without even knowing there's a problem. Then one day you wake up with a toothache. When you look back at your habits, you realize that you created the toothache.

It's the same with your life. You have created where you are right now by following your habits. The question is whether your habits have gotten you what you wanted, or whether you are living with the habits that no longer serve you.

The following concept comes from Bob Proctor, but is in my own words and understanding.

The conscious mind is everything in our awareness: what we think about, what we observe, where we make decisions, where we do our thinking, etc. It can process about forty bits of information a second. It filters the information coming in and keeps what you believe. It can accept or reject any idea based on your belief system.

The subconscious mind is the powerhouse inside of you. It runs the body, muscle movement, breathing, digestion, homeostasis, things of that nature. It is also where your habits and emotions are. It has no filters. It accepts new information without judgment. It can process about twenty million bits of information per second. That is five hundred thousand times faster than the conscious mind. It picks up everything. Your conscious mind can't do that.

Let's look at an example. You were talking to someone and got a funny feeling. You liked what the person was saying, but something didn't jive. That was your subconscious mind telling you that the person's body language and tonality didn't match the words. Because the subconscious mind can process information so much faster than the conscious mind, it picks up the incongruities. The conscious mind makes the decisions, but the subconscious mind runs your life.

We all have habits that put us on autopilot. Take a moment and think about yours. Do you have good habits and bad ones? What about those habits that are unproductive? What habits should you break? When I took the time to think about this, I realized there were habits that had to go and ones that had to be made. How about you? (wb) Choose a new belief and take action.

One of the habits I had to get rid of was negative self-talk. Negative self-talk is one of the most devastating plagues that consumes our world today. It's at the heart of violence, abuse, suicide, bullying, and many other destructive problems. It is the number one cause of low self-esteem. It does not matter what others say to you if you don't believe it! The problem arises when someone validates what you think is true. When you say disempowering things to yourself, others confirm what you have already decided on. It is not that your parents or peers create your self-esteem, they just add bricks to the belief you were already building. You create your own self-esteem. That is why it is called *self*-esteem.

Self-esteem is when you care about yourself and your place in the world. It's a decision you make concerning your value. It's knowing who you are inside, your strengths and weaknesses. It is a gift you give yourself every moment. The problem occurs when it is a gift you don't want. When you talk about yourself in a demeaning, degrading way, you lower your personal value.

You may be asking why personal value is so important. The answer I have found through my search for understanding is that I must value myself so I can live the life I was created for. You were created for a specific purpose. You have a place that no one else can fill. You are unique. There is not a single person in this universe that is like you. Stop talking down to yourself and start lifting yourself up so that others can follow. You were born an original. Stop trying to be a copy of someone else. When you treasure yourself, you live a life that is valuable.

Think about something you place high value on. Now write a list of at least thirty valuable things, and look for the common thread. (wb) If you are like most people, the common thread is how much the items cost. Now think about how you treat the items on your list They likely have a special place in your home. You probably know where they are and what condition they are in. They are usually kept clean and tidy. You may use these things only on special occasions. You treat them with care and the utmost respect and make sure others treat them the same way.

Think about the low-cost items you use every day. The things that are easy to replace. They get broken and dirty and thrown away. They get placed in a junk drawer with everything else that is of little value. You have an idea where you can find them, but you have to go and look.

It works the same way with you. If you treasure, aka value, yourself, you treat yourself as a rare jewel. You are the most precious item there is because you are the only one there is. You cannot be replaced. You wouldn't throw away one hundred pounds of gold. You wouldn't yell at it or call it names. You wouldn't put it in the corner and forget about it. You wouldn't let someone else take it and do what they wanted with it. Of course not!

Then why would you do that with your life? You can replace gold, but you cannot replace you. This is why valuing yourself is so important. When you value yourself, you treat yourself and everyone around you differently. When you respect your life, you can respect others. You would never hurt another valuable person. There is a built-in safety mechanism inside every human being. Humans cannot hurt other humans. Humans hurt objects and things. That is what bullies do; they hurt objects. They don't think of you as a human. They dehumanize you by calling you names. You become an object or a thing that they can hurt.

Some people get their personal value from modeling others. We spend a large part of the beginning of our lives observing others. The subconscious stores all the information it gathers and you draw on it when you fill a need or want. For example, if I were to say to you, "You are beautiful," what would you think? However you answered gives you an understanding of where your personal value is. You should always feel good when you receive a compliment, and always thank that person for giving you one. That is how they feel. If you negate what they have just said to you, you are disrespecting them and calling them a liar.

Harness the power of your mind to create the life you want. Whatever you focus on, you become. You tell yourself who and what you are. *You tell yourself*. Choose to tell yourself things that help you and make you better.

The wonderful thing about your marvelous mind is that you can change it whenever you want to. If you want to have a higher personal value and you would you like to be treated as the priceless valuable person you are, it starts with you and how you treat yourself. For the next few days, keep a journal of what you say to yourself (wb)—all those little comments you make about the things you do or don't do. Sometimes we think we have a good self-esteem and then find out we are actually saying very rude things to ourselves. Keep the journal (wb)—you need accurate information.

Now that you have current and accurate data about your self-talk and a good understanding of your personal value, evaluate it. Consider what the benefits would be if your human value was high, and how your life and the lives of those around you would change if you valued yourself more. This has nothing to do with ego. This is about the intrinsic value of a human and what that life means to the world. Valuing your life allows others to value theirs. Abuse, violence, murder, and hate crimes would all go away. You would never have to worry about yourself or a loved one being hurt by someone. What freedom you would rejoice in at having no fear of others. What a better world it would be, and it all starts with you liking yourself. Make the decision every day to like yourself, and watch how things change in your world.

You create your future. The habits you create determine what your future is like. You don't just enter the future, you create it with your actions. Take a moment to think about your current habits. Do they get you closer to your goals? Do you follow through with things that need to be done? Do you fill your time with productive activity? Are you on the path to what you desire, or are you drifting away? The sooner you catch your deviation off-course, the easier it will be to correct. The longer you go without course correction, the further off course you'll become. It takes small, easy adjustments every day. The space shuttle gets to the moon even though it is off course 90 percent of the time. The people responsible for the space shuttle constantly measure, monitor, and adjust its heading so it arrives at the destination. You need to do the same thing.

Carol Tuttle, the spiritual teacher, says, "Life is a mirror reflecting back at us what we believe about ourselves." When you change how you feel about yourself, others will change what they think about you as well. You are valuable not because someone tells you that you are, but because you decide to be. You are successful because you set a goal and worked at it. You made a decision and took action to make it so. You can do the same with your mind: harness it and make it work for you, not against you.

You may wonder what this has to do with bully proofing. Let me tie it together for you. You decide whether you like yourself or not. Other people's opinions verify what you already believe to be true. You either accept or reject the things they say depending on what you believe. If you have decided to have good personal value, you listen to the compliments of others. If you have decided to not like yourself, you only listen to the negative things that are said. What others say only has an impact to the extent you allow it. You control whether you are bullied or not by the importance you place on the would-be bully's opinion of you. If you think the opinion is important, you will place a higher value on it and allow it to affect you. You must decide that your opinion is more important than anyone else's.

Step one in bully proofing is to make a decision to like yourself, to realize you are important just because of who you are. Take a moment to make a list of one hundred reasons why you are valuable (wb)—no repeating. Read your list at least once a day in a place where you are relaxed and feel good. Let it fill you with pride and self-worth. Hold that feeling with you always. Choose to accept the belief that you are valuable and important in this wonderful world.

Perhaps you think this is all well and good for others, but your family and friends don't believe this new way of thinking. Then it's time to look outside your realm of comfort for new beliefs. They are out there—you just need to open up to them so you can be aware of the differences. If you've ever wanted something because it was unique and special, you might have noticed that item everywhere once you got it. The reason for this is awareness. You weren't looking for it before, so you weren't aware of it. It was outside of your consciousness. Your subconscious was aware of it; you were not. Your decision brought it into your consciousness or your awareness. The same will happen with deciding to change your values and beliefs. You will find people who believe it's important to love themselves and their beliefs will support you in your time of transition.

When you make a decision to change, you will have times when you're tempted to return to old habits. You'll have moments when you look back at what you left behind and wonder if you should return. Be ready to remind yourself why you decided to change. You are turning from a negative lifestyle to a more positive one, one in which you have more integrity and believe that nice guys do finish first. When you struggle to make a difference, to go against the crowd you have been hanging out with, remember why you are doing it.

One of my former students from Summit High School was a gang member. When he came to my class, he was facing tough charges. He was a big kid, about six-foot-four 275 pounds. He was tough and let everyone know it. He wanted revenge for the murder of a fellow gang member. I told him that hatred was like taking poison and expecting the other person to drop dead. It would never happen. He didn't believe me, so I took him through an exercise I do with my participants when they are stuck. I showed him how his body was weakened by his thoughts. I performed the exercise three more times and, each time, his body was weakened by his thoughts of revenge. It proved to him that his thoughts affect his physical body. He changed over the next few months, and when he went home, he was different. I also know he had a tough road ahead of him, and I like to believe he made it. If you keep focused on what you really want, you will succeed.

Take a moment and think about what you want for your life. If money were no object, would you move to a nicer place? Would you go to school? Would you hang out with different people? Would you quit your job and go to work someplace nicer? Would you travel? What would you do? (wb)

Now here is the tricky part. It's not about the money—it's about the mindset. It's about your perspective. How many times in the last week have you said, "I can't do that because _____." Or "I have to do _____." That's not really true. You choose to do or not to do things based on your beliefs. Consider how your life would change if you changed your belief around a matter and took action toward something you wanted.

Let's use the hypothetical belief of "I had bad things happen to me when I was younger, and so this is how I am now." You can come up with one of your own. I'm going to challenge this belief and the resulting person you have become because of it, so you might want to start with one that's easier for you to confront.

The reason I'm choosing the belief "bad things happened to me" is Elizabeth Smart, whose story made national headlines. When she was fourteen, she was kidnapped from her bedroom and forced to be the second wife of a man she didn't even know. She was later saved and is now living her life on her terms. She is not a victim anymore. She is strong and living her life to the fullest.

T. Harv Eker, an author and motivational speaker, says, "You can have reasons or results, but you can't have both." It's true. You can make excuses for where you are, or you can make different decisions and get the results you want. It's all about perspective and how we believe things are.

Here's another story to illustrate my point. It comes from the *Washington Post*.

In Washington DC, at a Metro station, on a cold January morning in 2007, a man with a violin played six Bach pieces for about forty-five minutes. During that time, approximately two thousand people went through the station, most of them on their way to work. After about three minutes, a middle-aged man noticed that there was a musician playing. He slowed his pace and stopped for a few seconds, and then he hurried on to meet his schedule. About four minutes later, the violinist received his first dollar. A woman threw money in the hat and, without stopping, continued to walk. At six minutes, a young man leaned against the wall to listen to him, then looked at his watch and started to walk again. At ten minutes, a three-year old boy stopped, but his mother tugged him along hurriedly. The kid stopped to look at the violinist again, but the mother pushed hard and the child continued to walk, turning his head the whole time. This action was repeated by several other children, but every parent—without exception—forced their children to move on quickly. At forty-five minutes, while the musician played continuously, only six people had stopped and listened for a short while. About twenty gave money but continued to walk at their normal pace. The man collected a total of thirty-two dollars. After an hour, he finished playing and silence took over. No one noticed and no one applauded. There was no recognition at all.

The violinist was Joshua Bell, one of the greatest musicians in the world. He played one of the most intricate pieces ever written, with a violin worth three and one-half million dollars. Two days before, Joshua Bell had sold out a theater in Boston where the seats averaged one hundred dollars each. He played the same music in the subway he had played in the Boston Theater.

Joshua Bell's incognito performance in the DC metro station was organized by the *Washington Post* as part of a social experiment about perception, taste, and people's priorities. My belief is that people did not expect to see a world-class musician in the subway. They weren't looking for it, so they didn't recognize it for what it was. They received something of great value for free and rejected it because of their beliefs. What are *your* beliefs costing *you*? (wb)

It is time to believe in yourself. It is time to take persistent, continuous action toward the attainment of your dreams. It is time to get moving forward and keep moving forward.

To recap what you have learned:

You decide what you believe.

You find situations that support your beliefs.

You take action based on your beliefs.

You can change your beliefs.

You make a decision to change.

You take new actions based on your new values.

You can look for situations to support your new belief.

You can live a more productive, harmonious life.

What you want to remember:

3

I LOVE MYSELF

"You are always a valuable, worthwhile human being, not because you're successful, ...but because you decide to know it."
— *Sally Northway Ogden*

I love myself. Why does society believe those words are wrong to say? Why do some people get upset when their children say them? It is time to turn the *Titanic* around and let everyone know that loving themselves is just fine. Bully proofing starts with self-love. It starts with feeling valuable and needed. Young children love themselves. They don't have problems with their identities until they are about ten years old and start to hear they are different from others. Well-meaning adults worry about these wonderful children not fitting in and being made fun of, so they tell them not to say such things, as it will get them in trouble or make them targets. It is time to educate you to a new way of thinking.

Self-love is also known as self-preservation. If I love myself, I will care for myself. I find value in my life and the talents I bring with me. The phrase, "Clean up your own front lawn and the world will be a better place" is true.

If we all found value in ourselves, we wouldn't try to take others down in order to lift ourselves up.

There are different reasons for bullying that we'll get into later, but right now we'll address leveling. Leveling is what happens when the players in the equation are no longer on the same level. For example, if I feel you are higher than I am, I will bring you down so we are even again. Some people call it the "crab in the bucket" syndrome. No one gets out because others keep pulling them back in.

If I love myself, then I don't care what others say because I still love myself. When someone says something hateful to me, the words have no impact because I have decided to love myself. The only time words affect me is when I already believe what is being said. My conscious mind has a filter to accept or reject whatever is not congruous with my beliefs. I preserve myself by choosing what I listen to.

During the safety briefing on an airplane, you are told to always put your oxygen mask on first. Once your mask is in place, you can then help others. It is the same with self-love. You have to love yourself before you can give love to others. You must accept yourself before you can accept others. If you don't like yourself, you won't believe someone who tells you, "I love you." Your subconscious says, "How can you love me when I don't feel worthy of love?" You reject the love. You are trying to get your needs met from an out-side force, when they need to be met within you. No one can make you feel loved or needed. You have to believe that you are. You have to love yourself first to accept love from others. You have to feel all of your emotions.

Picture a rainbow with some of the colors missing. If you had never seen one with all its colors, you wouldn't know what was missing. You would believe you were seeing the whole rainbow. You probably wouldn't believe someone who told you that part of your rainbow was missing. If you put on special glasses so you could see all the beautiful colors, your life would change. I hope you wouldn't be willing to give up your new glasses that let you see so much. That is what I offer you here: a new way of seeing the world and your place in it. You are loved and valued beyond measure. If you have loved ones, you know what I mean. You want only the best for them. You want to protect them. You want them to have a better life than you did, and you have passed on your knowledge to help them. Now *you* have new knowledge. You have to try it out for yourself. Start loving yourself today. Start valuing yourself. Treat yourself like the treasure you are. Remember that you are priceless, one of a kind, and irreplaceable, but you must feel it first. When you realize your value, the value of others goes up automatically.

As you lift yourself up, others come with you. You are the example of what their lives can become. Your vibration changes and you attract others. Try putting a smile on your face and walking down the street. See what happens to those you pass. Most will smile back. Those are the ones you have impacted positively. Focus on them.

Dr. Jeff Magee, author, speaker, and mentor says, "Ten percent of the people will love you and 10 percent will hate you. It doesn't matter what you do. It's the 80 percent in the middle you need to market to." So market to them with a smile on your face and a spring in your step.

My mom always said, "You catch more bees with honey than with vinegar.". When you're nice, people want to be a part of that. If you can ease their pain for just a moment with a smile, why not do it? A smile doesn't cost you anything, and it does so much good. Give strangers your beautiful smiles today, because that may be the only sunshine they see. Then tell yourself, "I did that and I'm proud of it." Be proud of who you are and what you can do. Be you so that others can be them. When you step into your power it allows others to claim theirs.

When you show respect and love to yourself, others will also. You teach people how to treat you. If you don't value yourself, they won't either. I know a lady who got so upset with her husband for calling her fat that she wanted a divorce. I told her, "I can't see what the problem is. You're the one who taught him that is how you want to be treated by calling yourself fat all the time." She said it was different when he did it. I asked her how.

Take a look at how you treat yourself and then at how others treat you. Is it time to make a change? It starts with you and a conversation with those closest to you. Let them know you would like their support in making a change. Then take action.

Start saying nice things about yourself. Make a list of your strengths and ask for help with your weaknesses. I gave a presentation at a high school and I asked the students who was good at math. Many of them raised their hands. I then asked them if they had offered help to others in their math classes. I challenged them to let others know they would love to help anyone who was having a hard time in exchange for help with something they needed. If we allow our children to be good at something, they can help others. It is a proven fact that you cannot help someone else without helping yourself. What a great way to make the world a better place, starting with your front yard.

When we are full of love, we can give some away. When we are lacking, we have to take. Think of all the blessings you have. Make a list of one hundred and no repeating. (wb) You'll feel unstoppable. This raises you to an entirely new level that makes you want to succeed. Now go out and bless others to help your newfound self grow and mature. Stay away from anyone who could hurt you. Like a new seedling trying to grow, your new self-esteem and personal value need protection. You must help and nurture them. Read books and talk to others who are where you want to be. Follow in the footsteps of those who have gone before. There are plenty. The appendix at the end of the book lists some. Make sure you are a generous giver and an excellent receiver.

T. Harv Eker taught me that to have a giver, you must have a receiver. I was of the false belief that it was better to give then to receive. How crazy is that? He's right. Giving and receiving are two sides of the same coin. You can't have a giver if there is no one to give to. The original statement is: it is better to be in a position to give than to be in a position where you have to receive. When you love yourself, you can give love to others. When you respect yourself, you can respect others at a new depth. When you are happy with yourself, you can be happy with others.

When you try to be what someone else wants, you are not yourself and it doesn't fit. It's like my daughter trying to wear my clothes. She is five-foot-ten and 135 pounds while I am six feet and 185 pounds. It will never work. She has to be her and I have to be me. That is the way it was planned.

Find out who you want to be, what you want to do, and then figure out the how. Research the people you like and why you like them. Bring those qualities into your life. Don't try to become them, because you can't. You can only become a better you. You get to create you. How amazing is that? Many people think they are born a certain way and never try to change. They just react to what is happening to them, never realizing they could create what they want. Ask yourself whom you should become, and then become it. Live the life you desire with the things that bring you joy. Stand up for who you are and what you want. I did not say step on others. I just said that you can choose to go your way, and they can go theirs. Start living your life.

The following story was written by Erma Bombeck right after she was diagnosed with breast cancer.

Take Time to Smell the Roses

Erma Bombeck

Too many people put off the things that bring them joy just because they haven't thought about it, don't have it on their schedules, didn't know it was coming, or are too rigid to depart from their routines.

I got to thinking one day about all those people on the Titanic *who passed up dessert at dinner that fateful night in an effort to cut back. From then on, I've tried to be a little more flexible.*

How many women out there will eat at home because their husband didn't suggest going out to dinner until after something had been thawed? Does the word "refrigeration" mean nothing to you?

How often have your kids dropped in to talk and sat in silence while you watched Law and Order *on television?*

I cannot count the times I called my sister and said, "How about going to lunch in a half hour?" She would stammer, "I can't. I have clothes in the washer. My hair is dirty. I wish I had known yesterday, I had a late breakfast," and my personal favorite: "It's Monday." She died a few years ago. We never did have lunch together.

Because Americans cram so much into their lives, we tend to schedule our headaches. We live on a sparse diet of promises we make to ourselves when all the conditions are perfect!

We'll go back and visit the grandparents when we get Steve toilet trained. We'll entertain when we replace the living-room carpet. We'll go on a second honeymoon when we get two more kids out of college.

Life has a way of accelerating as we get older. The days get shorter and the list of promises to ourselves gets longer. One morning, we awaken, and all we have to show for our lives is a litany of "I'm going to," "I plan on," and "Someday, when things are settled down a bit."

When anyone calls my "seize the moment" friend, she is open to adventure and available for trips. She keeps an open mind on new ideas. Her enthusiasm for life is contagious. You talk with her for five minutes, and you're ready to trade your bad feet for a pair of Rollerblades and skip an elevator for a bungee cord.

My lips have not touched ice cream in ten years. I love ice cream. It's just that I might as well apply it directly to my stomach with a spatula and eliminate the digestive process. The other day, I stopped the car and bought a triple-decker. If my car had hit an iceberg on the way home, I would have died happy.

Now...go on and have a nice day. Do something you want to...not something on your should-do list. If you were going to die soon and had only one phone call you could make, whom would you call and what would you say? And why are you waiting?

Have you ever watched kids playing on a merry-go-round or listened to the rain lapping on the ground?

Ever followed a butterfly's erratic flight or gazed at the sun into the fading night?

Do you run through each day on the fly? When you ask, "How are you?" Do you hear the reply?

When the day is done, do you lie in your bed with the next hundred chores running through your head?

Ever told your child, "We'll do it tomorrow." And in your haste, not seen his sorrow?

Ever lost touch? Let a good friendship die? Just call to say "Hi?"

When you worry and hurry through your day,
it is like an unopened gift...thrown away...

Life is not a race. Take it slower.
Hear the music before the song is over.

Life may not be the party we hoped for...but while we are
here we might as well dance!

Think about what you really want, what would cause you to wake up each morning and say, "I love me." Focus on that and then take the first step toward it. Every day, take one more step. The first few are the hardest, and then it gets easier. If you take a step every day, no matter how small, you make progress. You develop momentum and then you are unstoppable. When fear and doubt creep in, banish them with feelings of hope and faith. Keep your eye on your dream, keep your feet moving forward, and make it happen. Look to others that have gone before you so they can encourage you and give you strength. Remember that what one person can do, you can do too. There is no pain greater than the pain of regret. You can live your life so you have no regrets if you want to. It just takes making a decision and then taking the actions required to put it in place. You don't have to know the how, you just need to define your why: why you must live the life you have dreamed of creating. When your why is big enough, you can overcome anything.

I got the following story in an e-mail some time ago. It is about a father's love and how it overcomes monstrous obstacles.

Some years ago, on a hot summer day in south Florida, a
little boy decided to go for a swim in the old swimming hole
behind his house. In a hurry to dive into the cool water, he
ran out the back door, leaving behind shoes, socks, and shirt
as he went. He flew into the water, not realizing that as he
swam toward the middle of the lake, an alligator was swim-
ming toward the shore.

His father, working in the yard, saw the two as they got closer and closer together. In utter fear, he ran toward the water, yelling to his son as loudly as he could.

Hearing his dad's voice, the little boy became alarmed and made a U-turn to swim to his father. It was too late. Just as he reached his father, the alligator reached him. From the dock, the father grabbed his little boy by the arms as the alligator snatched his legs. That began an incredible tug-of-war between the two. The alligator was much stronger than the father, but the father was much too passionate to let go. A farmer happened to drive by, heard the screams, raced from his truck, took aim, and shot the alligator.

Remarkably, after weeks and weeks in the hospital, the little boy survived. His legs were extremely scarred by the vicious attack of the animal. And on his arms were deep scratches where his father's fingernails dug into his flesh in his effort to hang on to the son he loved.

The newspaper reporter who interviewed the boy after the trauma asked the boy if he would show him his scars. The boy lifted his pant legs. And then, with obvious pride, he said to the reporter, "But look at my arms. I have great scars on my arms too. I have them because my dad wouldn't let go."

I'm sure that if you had asked the father earlier that morning if he could save his son from an alligator, he would have had doubts. However, in the moment, he was able to do whatever it took to preserve his son's life. He didn't worry about what would happen after. He just knew that if he let go, his son would die. His why was so big he was able to find the how.

Your life may not be in this kind of turmoil. You may not have anything as bad as an alligator snapping at your heels, but you just aren't very happy. If you are not living the life you were made for, it will be difficult to feel inner peace and happiness. When you are aligned with your life's mission, it shines on your face and in your eyes. You can't hide it, not that you'd want to. It shows people the love and abundance you have welling up inside. You have so much, you can give some away, and people need what you have.

Erma Bombeck said, "When I stand before God at the end of my life, I would hope that I would not have a single bit of talent left and could say, 'I used everything you gave me.'"

There is need of your voice. Don't hide it because of your fears of inadequacy. Let it be heard so you can be an example for others. Let others follow you, just as you have followed. Mahatma Gandhi said, "Be the change you wish to see in the world." Stop waiting for someone else to fix your problems and fix them yourself. You have the power and strength to make it so; you just have to take action.

Another story to illustrate my point.

The Cab Ride

Twenty years ago, I drove a cab for a living. One evening, taking a call at two-thirty in the morning, I found the building dark except for a single light in a ground-floor window. Under these circumstances, many drivers would just honk once or twice, wait a minute, and then drive away. But I had seen too many impoverished people who depended on taxis as their only means of transportation. Unless a situation smelled of danger, I always went to the door. This passenger might be someone who needed my assistance, I reasoned to myself.

So I walked to the door and knocked. "Just a minute," answered a frail, elderly voice. I could hear something being dragged across the floor.

After a long pause, the door opened. A small woman, looking to be in her eighties, stood before me. She wore a print dress and a pillbox hat with a veil pinned on it, like someone out of a 1940s movie. By her side was a small nylon suitcase. The apartment looked as if no one had lived in it for years. All the furniture was covered with sheets. There were no clocks on the walls, no knickknacks or utensils on the counters. In the corner was a cardboard box filled with photos and glassware.

"Will you carry my bag out to the car?" she said.

I took the suitcase to the cab, and then returned to assist the woman. She took my arm and we walked slowly toward the cab.

She kept thanking me for my kindness.

"It's nothing," I told her. "I just try to treat my passengers the way I would want my mother treated."

"Oh, you're such a good boy," she said.

When we got in the cab, she gave me an address, and then asked, "Could you drive through downtown?"

"It's not the shortest way," I reminded her.

"Oh, I don't mind," she said. "I'm in no hurry. I'm on my way to a hospice."

I looked in the rearview mirror. Her eyes glistened.

"I don't have any family left," she continued. "The doctor says I don't have very long."

I quietly reached over and shut off the meter. "What route would you like me to take?" I asked.

For the next two hours, we drove through the city. She showed me the building where she had once worked as an elevator operator. We drove through the neighborhood where she and her husband had lived when they were newlyweds. She had me pull up in front of a furniture warehouse that had once been a ballroom where she had gone dancing as a girl. Sometimes she'd ask me to slow in front of a particular building or corner and would sit staring into the darkness, saying nothing.

As the first hint of sun creased the horizon, she suddenly said, "I'm tired. Let's go now."

We drove in silence to the address she had given me. It was a low building, like a small convalescent home, with a driveway that passed under a portico. Two orderlies came out to the cab as soon as we pulled up. They were solicitous and intent, watching her every move. They must have been expecting her.

I opened the trunk and took the small suitcase to the door. The woman was already seated in a wheelchair.

"How much do I owe you?" she asked, reaching into her purse.

"Nothing," I said.

"You have to make a living," she insisted.

"There are other passengers," I told her.

Almost without thinking, I bent and gave her a hug. She held onto me tightly.

"You gave an old woman a little moment of joy," she said "Thank you."

I squeezed her hand and then walked into the dim morning light. Behind me, a door shut. It was the sound of the closing of a life.

The rest of that shift, I didn't pick up any more passengers. I drove aimlessly, lost in thought. For the rest of that day, I could hardly talk. What if that woman had gotten an angry driver or one who was impatient to end his shift? What if I had refused to take the run, or had honked once and then driven away? On quick review, I don't think that I have ever done anything more important in my life.

So often we think it's the big decisions that will have the largest impact on us. Maybe that is why we spend so much time thinking about them and trying so hard to make the correct ones. Many times, it's the small, day-to-day ones that shape our lives. When you feel that little pull or hear that small voice telling you to do something, maybe you should. It might be the thing you need to get you were you want to go. What do you have to lose? Your way has gotten you where you are. You want to go someplace else. It's time to take a different path. It's time to love yourself and make a difference.

To recap your learning:

Step one to bully proofing is raising your personal value.

When you love yourself, you give others permission to do the same.

The change starts with you.

Follow your higher power when it comes to making decisions.

Take time to live your life to its fullest.

Always love yourself.

What you want to remember:

PERSPECTIVE

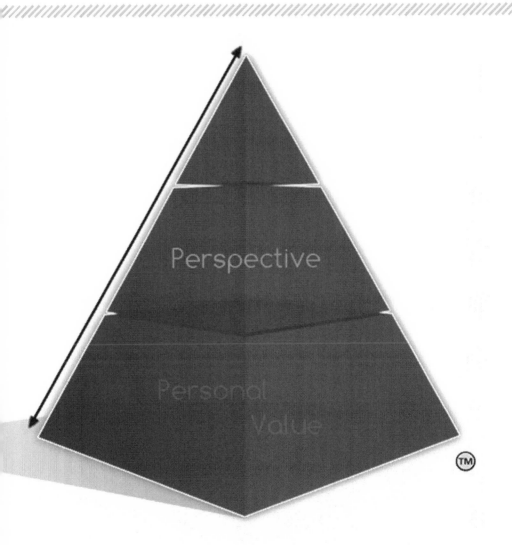

4

IT'S ABOUT THEM

"Your associations will either help or destroy you."
— *Sir Richard Branson*

One of the hardest points to remember when you are being bullied is that it's about the bully. The bullying is not about you. It's about the bully's pain and insecurities.

Think of a time when you were happy and things were going your way. You knew you were loved and valued. In this wonderful, happy place, could you hurt or lash out at anyone? No! You wanted to love and be loved. You were full, and you had some to share with others.

Now think of a time when you were hurt or sad. You were in a place where you wanted the pain to stop, and someone tried to cheer you up. It was easy to lash out, was it not? Maybe you felt bad about it later, but at the time, you just wanted that person to feel some of the pain you were feeling. This is where most bullies are coming from.

The definition of a bully is: a person who is habitually cruel to others who are weaker. This often takes the form of words that hurt or intimidate the victim. That is the type of bullying I am addressing.

First let's talk about words. Doug Nelson, #1 bestselling author and trainer, taught me that nothing has meaning except the meaning we give it. Words are just words. My interpretation of words gives them their meanings. I could say the word "anger" and it would bring up different feelings for you than it does for me. Emotional words can bring with them feelings of pain or pleasure. For example, I love the word *hon*. It brings back a powerful memory for me. At a time in my life when I was really struggling and wondering if I was making the right decisions, a waitress said it to me.

Let me explain.

It was raining, so I went into a Denny's in downtown Salt Lake City, Utah. I didn't have money to buy anything. I was a student at the University of Utah and carrying 21-27 credits at a time. I finished sixty-five credits in three terms so I could graduate that year. I was a single parent and working three part-time jobs to pay the rent, buy food, clothes, and books. I wondered if it was all worth it. I felt in my heart that if I could just finish my bachelor of science degree while Erin was young, she could have a better life. We could have a better life. Without an education, I knew I could not support her the way I wanted to. So there I sat one cold, rainy day, wondering if it was worth it. After work, homework, limited time with Erin, and classes, I got about three hours of sleep a night. I was tired, I was cold, and I didn't think I could go on. Then Grace, my waitress, came up to my table and said, "What can I get you, hon?" I looked at my hands and didn't say anything. She was my amazing Grace. She knew what was up. She patted my hand and said, "Don't you worry, hon. I'm going to take care of you." She brought me a hot roast beef sandwich and a glass of milk. I told her I couldn't pay. She said, "Just pay it forward." Ever since that day, I have loved the word *hon*.

I went on to get my bachelor of science degree. When I walked across that stage to receive my diploma, it really was worth all the struggles. I held my head up high and waved to my daughter and parents in the stands. If I could have done handsprings, I would have. I became a teacher because I wanted to help others get an education, just like Coach Pat Emerson and so many others had helped me.

I chose to teach at an alternative high school about two years into my career. I knew I wanted to help kids, and what better way than there? This alternative school is where students who are removed from mainstream schools go. My students were "at risk" of never graduating. Some were in gangs. Some were on drugs and most were in the state's custody. I loved my job and enjoyed helping them turn their lives around. I knew that when one of them changed, generations changed.

I had one student we'll call Timmy who was having a hard time. He and I wound up in the counselor's office one day. As we talked, it came out that he hated it when I called him "hon." I didn't understand because I loved that word and it meant so much to me. Timmy told me about his experience with *hon*.

Timmy had an older sister with some emotional issues. When she wanted something from him, she called him *hon*, and then proceeded to abuse him. Every time he heard the word *hon*, he learned that pain would follow.

It wasn't the word, it was what came with the word that mattered. I remembered pleasure; Timmy remembered pain. We both reacted to our feelings and the meanings we gave the word, and not to the word itself.

Think of some of the words that push your buttons or tighten your jaws. (wb) Now find out why you feel that way about them. Is it your past? Is it the fact that you have been told they are bad words and shouldn't be used? Once you figure out why you don't like them, you can take the power out of them. You have the choice to no longer let them affect you. You no longer have to be impacted by them.

I think one of the biggest disservices we do our children is to let them believe that words can hurt them. Remember that saying, "Sticks and stones may break my bones, but words will never hurt me." What about, "I'm rubber and you're glue. What you say bounces off me and sticks to you." What if you started teaching your children and those around you that they have the power to decide what impacts them? Society needs to stop telling us that a verbal attack is the most terrible thing that can happen. It's not! There are far worse things. Verbal bullying is just words. You must stop letting people you don't even like tell you how to feel about yourself. You must take your power back. You have the power to decide who you will be and what matters to you.

Bullies react to their environments. They are trying to survive and, in the process, want to keep others down as well. If they see you as being better than they are, they will strike out. They want everyone to feel as bad and uncertain as they do. They are coming from a place of fear, powerlessness, and hopelessness. They have to make sure that no one gets ahead of them. They don't see how their dreams will ever come true. They have given up and are making excuses for their lots in life. If you follow your dreams, it voids their excuses.

A few years ago Amanda Dickson, a speaker and radio show host, spoke at the Alpine School District's annual meeting. She validated my thoughts on this issue. She told us a story about how she had received an email from a man that was full of hate. She spoke of how much it hurt her and made her cry. She made the decision to reach out to him and through that touch she found out how hopeless he thought his life was. She found out that he needed help and had no idea how to ask for it. He was in pain and wanted everyone else to be as well. I remember thinking, "Amanda Dickson, a person that is so well liked she has a huge radio following, is receiving hate mail. How can that be?" It caused me to delve deeper into understanding why people do the things they do.

Your friends can accidently bully you as well. When you do well and move toward your dreams, they might try to stop you. They'll say they're trying to protect you. However, their fear of failure stops them, so they want it to stop you as well. If they stop you from moving forward, their belief that it cannot be done is validated, and they continue to be right. People go to great lengths to make sure their beliefs are correct. That is one of the reasons it is so important to know what yours are and how they affect you. You might just need to change them.

Seeing bullies as victims of their circumstances takes the pressure off of you. You no longer have to react to the words they say. Their words are just smoke screens the bullies hide behind. They want the pressure on you and off themselves so they can keep hiding from their unhappy lives.

What we discussed about choices is true here as well: you choose what you believe. People tell you how great you are. You are told you are good looking and smart. You are told you can do whatever you want to. The problem occurs when you choose to listen to the negative things people say, when you choose to be unhappy. When you choose to not listen to the positive comments.

If you or someone you love is dealing with a bully and you have let it affect you in the past, it is time to make a new decision and stop the pain. Choose to listen to the positive statements that come your way every day. Have hope for the future. Believe that things can change. You can lean on your faith in yourself and others. Like Grace in my story, someone is waiting to help you see the silver lining in your rain clouds. You will make it. You will survive if you choose to. You can change your perspective with one choice.

I moved schools a lot when I was young. I had to learn how to make friends quickly and easily; sometimes, I had a hard time keeping them once I moved. I would lose touch or we would just grow apart. I would change and not keep them up to date about my new likes, feelings, and activities.

I called a friend after not hearing from her for some time because I felt she had not kept in touch very well. I had gotten in the habit of her calling me every week. When she didn't for a few weeks, I called her to see why she hadn't called. She told me, "The phone line runs both ways." I realized that was true. I had gotten use to her calling me. She felt like a bother.

You see my friends perspective was one in which I had moved away. Mine was that she had. In reality, we both had. She became insecure and felt she was covering the distance and wanted me to do my part. I was glad we could talk about it and she told me how she was feeling.

While you're waiting for someone, life continues and a distance can grow. When you feel the pulling away, you might get more insecure and look to others to validate you. If they don't validate you the way you need, the distance grows and you feel more and more alone. You must recognize this downward spiral and pull yourself out of it. You must fill the holes in your heart from within; nothing from the outside will help. You won't listen to it anyway. When you don't believe you are worth anything, you don't listen when someone says you are. You must start looking for the positives in your life.

Go over the lists you made while reading this book. The one hundred things to be grateful for, the one hundred things you like about your life, and the one hundred things you have done that you are proud of. Then start looking for things to be happy about. (wb)

When I get up in the morning and my feet hit the floor, I say to myself, "I love my life." Then my subconscious goes about finding reasons why this is true. You need to set yourself up for success. Listen to the positive, uplifting things people say. Consider what you are listening to: what the song lyrics say about life, what the characters in the movies or on TV say about each other and themselves, and what your friends and family say to you or about you. Listen to words that lift you up and help you feel better about yourself and your life.

Take a moment and think about your friends. You are like your five closest friends. The reason is that they are in your comfort zone. You are OK with everything they do, or you will be soon. Think of yourself as an X in the middle of a circle, which represents your comfort zone. Fill the circle with everything you like. Put the things you like most right next to you, and put the things that are all right further away. Put the things you don't like on the outside of the circle, again in degrees of dislike around the outside of the circle. (wb) Notice the things that used to be on the outside of the circle that are now on the inside. (wb) Maybe you used to be afraid of the water, but now you swim. Or heights was an issue, but you have learned to rappel or taken up rock-climbing, so they are on the line or just inside it. You need to know what you surround yourself with on a daily basis so you can start to change it. If you don't know who you are and what you like, you can't expect to change. You need a starting point.

I am not making any judgment calls. It's your comfort zone, and you get to decide what is in it and what you keep out. I'm merely helping you become aware of your unconscious mind and how it controls your day-to-day life. Things that society considers good and bad, but you get the final say because you have to live with the consequences of your decisions.

Look at what is in your comfort zone. Perhaps it contains exercise, healthy eating, smoking, drinking alcohol, education, lying, stealing, giving 10 percent of your income away, lots of money, nice things, family, drugs, prison. Consider what you currently do or are comfortable with that you need to change.

Think again about what you like about your five best friends and if there is anything you would want to change. (wb) Then think about what you like about your life and what would you change if you could. List everything you would like to change, such as health, job, residence—where you live or the home itself—car, weight, habits, money you make, clothes, food. (wb)

The things you have are in your comfort zone. Things you want are outside your comfort zone because there is too much about them you don't know or understand. You want a nicer home, a newer car, or a better job, but you might be afraid of how your friends will react, so you keep things the same. If they drink, you drink. If they smoke, you smoke. If they don't like their jobs, you don't like yours. If they complain about their life, you complain about yours. You might not at first, but you do now because when that behavior was brought into your comfort zone, you didn't kick it out. Whatever you surround yourself with is what you are comfortable with, even if it means having people say things to you that are not so nice. Maybe it's time to start deciding what you want around you instead of settling.

The first time I stepped into a nice hotel was when my husband and I registered for a conference at the beautiful San Diego Hilton Resort and Spa in San Diego, California. I walked in the front door and wanted to walk right back out. I was that uncomfortable. I didn't think I belonged. The resort was amazing. There was marble and glass and beauty everywhere. I had never been around any of that. I grew up on a dairy farm in Washington state. We had stayed in a hotel about three times in my life, and they were never fancy. My mom made our clothes from hand-me-downs. We had a garden and canned or jarred most of our food. When I stepped into the foyer of that incredible resort, I was outside of my comfort zone. It was time to grow in a way I didn't even know existed. My husband, Laurence, talked with me and helped me understand what I was feeling.

Now I stay in nice hotels frequently, and it feels wonderful. I have brought nice things into my comfort zone.

Think about who and what you want to kick out of your comfort zone or bring into it. (wb) They may be out of your awareness and you can look to your friends and their lives to shine a light on yours. If you want to bring something new in, you can find people who already have it in their lives, and copy them.

If Helen Keller and Anne Sullivan did not have each other, we might never have heard of either one of them. The same with Abbot and Costello, or Seabiscuit, Red Pollard, Tom Smith, and Charles Howard. These winners all have something in common. They had a team of people that helped them succeed. Surround yourself with people that lift you up and help you reach your goals. Choose your friends—have a criterion they need to meet before you spend large amounts of time with them. You can think of it as a friend interview. You are giving them an important place in your future. Choose wisely.

Stop hanging out with people who give you a hard time or make you feel bad. Cut off all contact with anyone who cyberbullies you. Don't listen to or read what that person writes about you. Walk away or shut it off. You don't have to let it impact you in any way. *You* decide what it all means to you. You decide how important that person is in your life. You get to decide who is in your environment.

Remember that bullies are unhappy with their lives and want to make sure you are as well. They may also be using you as a scapegoat. Maybe they are mad at someone they are afraid to say anything to, but they can make you a target. They can say all kinds of things to you because you are not a threat, or because your opinion of them does not matter. They don't care if you are hurt or upset because you don't matter to their lives. They have enormous holes in their self-esteem. They don't like themselves so they don't care about you. However, you have made the decision that you are valuable, that you are here on a mission, and you have filled all of your holes with self-love and personal value. You can understand their pain and what they are going through because you were there once yourself. You can show them compassion by not getting involved in the drama they stir up. You know you are better than that. It doesn't matter what they say because you know differently. You can tell them, "Thank you." You don't have to tell them why, but in your heart, you are glad you are no longer like them. You have moved beyond that. You are powerful and strong in who you are and what you must do; their negative comments have no power over you. They are just reminders that there is still work to be done.

It's my mission to let everyone know they have a decision to make about their own value. In my trainings and presentations, I tell everyone, "You need to step into your power and create a life of significance. You must decide to be successful." Success is when you plot your direction and then take steps to make it happen. Success is something you choose. Where you are right now doesn't matter, only that you decide what you want and why you want it. There will be obstacles that pop up in your path. If your why is big enough, you will do whatever it takes to keep moving forward. There are many examples of people who never gave up. There are books about them, movies about them, people talk about them. We, as a society, don't glorify people who give up. Many people quit, but no one writes books about them. Look around you to see people who have quit and become dreamers. If you want to achieve, you must seek out people who are achievers. Read about them, study them, copy them when appropriate. You can learn how to overcome your obstacles by seeing how they overcame theirs. You must want it with a passion that will not be deterred. You must have courage to fight through your fears. You must have stamina to continue your course. You need a plan on what to do when naysayers show up.

Success doesn't just happen. You must be committed to making it happen. Your path will be distinct from others because you are starting from somewhere they did not. You have different challenges and impediments to overcome. You can use their example, but you must walk your own path. You must take action; you must create motion to travel your path to success. Elvis Presley grew up believing in a dream that he made a reality. His mottos were TCB (taking care of business) and FTD (follow that dream). They can be seen in much of his life and his home. He used physical reminders to help him correct his course when he got off track.

Physical reminders are things you use or see on a daily basis to remind you of what you want and where you are going. (wb) I use a necklace, ring, and bracelet. My clients use all kinds of objects that they carry with them or hang on their walls so they see them first thing in the morning. You can too. Pick something that reminds you of the new path you are on and put it in a prominent place. This will help remind you that you are valuable. Give yourself a chance to grow into your newfound self-esteem. When you first make the decision to like yourself, you might need to remind yourself of your value several times a day. That's OK. Just keep doing it.

My family put a big sticky note poster on the wall with the outline of a first-place trophy on it. Every time we said nice things about ourselves, we traced a one-inch line on the trophy. When it was filled in, we got dressed up and went out for a wonderful dinner at a fancy restaurant. Come up with your own way of celebrating your newfound personal value and, remember, when people say mean things to you, it's about them not you.

Let's revisit the main themes in this chapter:

You choose your perspective.

You can use pain or pleasure as a motivator.

Bullies have different reasons why they bully.

You can choose a life of love and abundance.

You can live a life of gratitude.

What you want to remember:

5

I FEEL YOUR PAIN

"You have the ability to understand what others are feeling if you look at it from their perspective."
— *Jeanie Cisco-Meth*

Let's talk about why people bully for a moment. Remember the definition we are using for this book: a person who is habitually cruel to others who are weaker. In other words, bullies are people who make a habit of being mean to others who they think won't stand up to them. We are talking about people, teens or adults, who intimidate others repeatedly. In chapter four, you learned that people bully because they are in pain and want you to be miserable as well.

Let's look at some other reasons why some people might feel the need to misbehave. First of all, our society gives a great deal of attention to people who behave badly. You see it all the time in the media: reality TV shows, headlines, YouTube videos, and movies. When people act outside of what is considered normal, some people view it as noteworthy and report or record it. Others watch it or read about it, so it is a way to make money.

The problem occurs when people start modeling the behavior because they think it is now the normal way to behave.

Statistics can play into this as well. When you hear a statistic like this one from the United States Department of Justice, "One in four teenagers is likely to be bullied in their adolescence," it sounds like everyone is being bullied. However if the statistic was written as three out of four teens might never be bullied, the perception would be totally different. Both show that 25 percent of the teen population might be bullied. The difference is where the focus is placed: on the teens who are being bullied or on the teens who are not.

People might also choose to bully because of jealousy and envy. They want to be more like their victims but see no way of attaining it. It might be the victim's good looks, better grades, more popularity, or better home life. They target you because they want to be like you but lack the social skills to become you.

Bullies might also feel justified or provoked in some way. They misunderstood something you said or did to either them or friends of theirs. They might be mad at you for some perceived slight. The best way to clear this kind of bullying up is a conversation between you and the bully.

One of the saddest reasons people bully is because of abuse at home. They are in so much pain, physically and mentally, and they have no hope of it ending. All they see in the future is more pain, so they strike out at those around them. This is a cry for help because they don't know what else to do. They might think their behavior is normal—it's the way they have been taught to deal with others. They live their life in fear.

Fear is the anticipation of pain. When you are afraid, you don't always behave in a rational manner, and you are more likely to lash out at others. Think about how you reacted the last time you were afraid. Probably not to the best of your ability. Think about your feelings after the fear passed. Imagine living in fear of your next beating and not even knowing why it might happen, or seeing your family members being hurt and you have no idea what to do about it. That might be the kind of life the person bullying you has.

Little children have no fear. Fear is a learned response due to past pain. Take children who are learning to walk. They don't have any fear of falling down or looking silly. They just know they want to walk. They watch Mom and Dad to see how it is accomplished and they set out to do it as well. They fall down and get up and try again. They keep trying until they can walk. Depending on how the parents react to the first fall, children can learn quickly with no fear or develop fear and proceed more cautiously. They must be taught about drop-offs and steps. They have to learn some fear so they don't continue to hurt themselves or get in real danger. Parents use the anticipation of pain to teach their children how to avoid it.

The anticipation of pain is what causes bullying to be so scary for the victim. The adrenal glands secrete adrenaline into your body and you freeze, get ready to run, or fight. Blood flow to the brain is decreased so you can't think very clearly; however, if you can remember that the bully might be in pain, maybe you can have some empathy or sympathy.

What is the difference between sympathy and empathy? Sympathy is feeling sorry for someone else, while empathy is putting yourself in that person's shoes. Either will help you deal with the verbal attack. If you can view the bully as a person in pain, you can deflect the attack. You won't allow the words to impact you because you know they are not about you or your family. The attack is about the bully expressing pain and despair. It is a cry for help. Maybe the bully doesn't know any better and just needs to be educated. When you feel either empathy or sympathy for the bully, you will not be as impacted by what is said. You are less likely to feel bad about yourself or to try and retaliate. Retaliation makes it worse because the bully gets what they want.

If your self-esteem is not strong enough to withstand some words from an angry person, then spend some time building it up. I gave many tips and tools on how to accomplish that in the first part of this book. When you have a healthy self-image, you have an attitude that things will be all right. You realize that whatever the bully said to hurt or intimidate you is not true, and you move on. You're glad it's not your life that is hopeless. Your attitude is one of faith and hope for the future. The bully's is one of despair and fear. Have some compassion for the bully and come from a place of love for your fellow man.

Your ability to care for others can grow like a muscle you exercise. Practice acceptance of others and you will get better at it. Remember when you've had a bad day and cut them some slack. When you do have a bad day, pull yourself up by sharing your love with someone else. When you help someone, you help yourself. Sit by someone new in the lunchroom, or help someone with homework without asking for anything in return. The rewards you receive are priceless. When you give freely, your spirit will lift and your heart will be full again. The key is to give. You must help without compensation. You won't know where your reward will come from, but it will come. Serve others with a good heart just for the purpose of helping them out. As you help others, you will find your life is fuller and richer than it was before.

This is a big change from what society teaches. People who have chosen to blame others for their places in life are in the news. They point at others and say, "It's my parents' fault I'm like this," or, "I was bullied and that is why I decided to hurt or kill others." You must be one of the powerful change agents for good. You must stand up and let people know that what they say about you doesn't impact you unless you decide to let it. Your life and the lives of those around you will start to change. Change takes a while to become permanent so stick with it.

When you change it takes time to reap the harvest. You reap the harvest from the seeds of the past. You must plant new seeds so you can reap a new harvest. Start doing more for others, and watch what your future holds. You don't know the germination period, but don't get discouraged.

Keep up the good work and have faith. Be open and ready to receive. Your compensation for your kind decision is on the way. What will you do with it?

You can also help by stopping bullying before it occurs. Look for people who need a friend, and be a friend to them. Look for kids who sit alone at lunch or walk with their heads down in the hallway. These are signs of low self-esteem and maybe you can help them. Start a conversation to determine the person's interests. You might be interested in it as well or know someone who is, and you can help the two meet each other. Look for people that might be lonely and talk to them. Ask how they like the school and their classes. Again, find out if you have anything in common. Maybe your friendship is all they need to turn their lives around. Make sure you are curious and not condemning. If you approach them with condemnation in your voice, they will hear it. Communication is 93 percent body language and tonality. If you are anything but curious, they might be defensive and you will never get to know them. Be interested in them and what they need and want. Zig Ziglar, author, salesman, and motivational speaker, said, "If you help enough people get what they want, you will get what you want." It is so true. It is karma coming around again.

If they seem open to help or discussion, you can educate them about bullying and how it affects your environment. Ask them how they think they can help. Don't accuse them of bullying. Just educate them about the problem. Let them know you are trying to help other kids so that no one is afraid to come to school or work, and ask them if they have any ideas. Talk to them about different ways to relieve stress and how you'd like to teach others. Tony Robbins, author and trainer, got his start in high school. Students came to him and asked his advice in many areas. He always helped them. You could do the same. You could help make your school and workplace a safer, better place to be. Our world needs more positive leaders and you might be the one who stops the fallout of bullying.

Learning healthful ways of dealing with stress is important. Everyone has stress, and it can ruin your life if you don't learn how to deal with it. Here are some ideas that help:

1. Find a hobby you enjoy
    a. Woodworking
    b. Painting
    c. Sewing
    d. Sculpting
    e. Gardening
    f. Singing
2. Exercise
    a. Walk
    b. Run
    c. Lift weights
    d. Aerobics
    e. Zumba
    f. Sports
3. Read a book
4. Talk to a friend
5. Help someone else

This is just a list to get you started. There are other things you can do as well. Make a list of things you can do to relieve your stress. (wb)

We feel stress when we encounter new experiences. When you grow and can handle the new situation, the stress goes away. Think about growing and becoming a more significant person so that you are no longer stressed by the new circumstance. As you mature and become better able to handle more stress, you grow as a person and so does your paycheck. Stop wishing for less stress and find a way to expand so that it no longer stresses you. You want the capacity to handle whatever comes your way.

In the beginning, this new way of thinking will cause you stress. Let's return to the conscious and unconscious mind we discussed earlier in this book. Bob Proctor, world thought leader, says that when a new idea comes into your conscious mind, it causes disharmony. Let's say you have an X way of thinking. If you believe it, your body and mind are in harmony. It doesn't cause you stress. Then you are introduced to a new idea, Y. You think it will make your life better. However, until you accept Y and kick X out, or you stay with X and kick Y out, you will have stress.

Let me walk you through an example.

Let's say you are happy with your eating habits (X thinking). You eat at McDonald's three times a day, and sometimes four. In a health class or in a book or in the news, you learn that eating fried, greasy foods like McDonald's is not good for you and can cause many health-related issues. This is the introduction of Y thinking. The next time you head to McDonald's to eat, you think about this new information, and it causes you stress. You need to decide if you will accept the new way of eating, or stay with the old. Until you make the decision, you have stress because the old programming and the new programming, X and Y, are in disharmony.

You go through the same pattern with any new programming that is introduced. People who are in disharmony tend to strike out at others because of the stress they feel. They may become bullies because they have no idea how to deal with this disharmony. If you are also stressed, the bullying instance can be even worse because of how you handle it. At any other time, you might choose to walk away, but this time you fight back, and that leads to even more stress because of the consequences you now face. Remember, stress is a choice. It is you accepting or rejecting a new idea. When you are presented with a new idea, research it and decide what you believe quickly. This will help lower your stress levels and you can ease through life more gracefully.

If you feel overwhelmed, get help. There are many people you can speak with who are waiting to assist you in whatever you might need. If you want help dealing with stress, talk to a counselor or someone who is qualified to help in that area. If you would like to help someone who is being bullied, offer a copy of this book. You can also have the victim talk to qualified personnel. You must protect yourself. You are valuable. Your presence on this planet is needed. You are not more valuable than anyone else, but you are valuable and must treat yourself and others as such. Make sure you take care of yourself: get plenty of sleep, eat nutritious meals, drink water, exercise at least three times a week, and enjoy life and all it has to offer. Life is an adventure to be lived. Stop watching TV and playing video games and live a life filled with experiences that are worth talking about. Choose to be yourself and grow more every day.

Get to know people. They might have the answers you've been looking for. Maybe they can help you understand a new concept. They might be dealing with some pretty horrendous things in their lives and you can be glad you don't have their problems. It's all a matter of perspective.

An acquaintance of mine, who I'll call Lisa, told me the following story. As Lisa was riding Trax light-rail public transportation to work one morning, she had an experience that changed her perspective about others. She lived by the hospital and her ride was about forty-five minutes long. She enjoyed riding Trax because she didn't have to deal with parking, and she could read a good book. She had been on the train for about five minutes when a father got on with his four children, who ranged in ages from about ten to three. They all looked like they had slept in their clothes because their clothing was rumpled and dirty. They hadn't had a shower for a few days and smelled a little ripe.

The children sat quietly for a few moments and then grew restless. They started pushing one another, and then they started talking. As the pushing increased, so did the volume of their voices. The father sat there as though nothing was going on. He never once said anything to his children. Pretty soon the kids were chasing each other around the train. Still the father didn't say anything.

Other passengers got upset because their day was being disrupted. They were used to riding to work in silence. They'd read, work on their laptops, listen to music, look out the window, or talk quietly with their neighbors. It was usually civilized and mannerly, not like that morning at all. They gave the father and his children looks that said, "What are you doing? Can't you see you are bothering us?" The father never raised his eyes from the floor and the children had no clue what was going on. The tension continued to mount.

Then one man in a dark blue suit stood up and walked over to the father. You could hear the sigh of relief. Everyone thought the disruption would end. The man in the suit cleared his throat and the father seemed to shake himself and come out of a deep trance. The father looked up at the nicely dressed man with a question in his gaze. The man in the suit asked the father, "Can you not hear and see what your children are doing on this train? You need to control them. They are bothering everyone else."

The father, with a sad expression on his face, looked at his children with love in his eyes. They immediately quieted down and came to him. He didn't say a word. He put his arms around them and, with tears running down his face, he said, "We are all out of sorts this morning. I decided to take the train home because I didn't trust myself to drive. You see, my wife, their mother, died this morning and we just don't know what we are going to do. I'm sure we'll figure it out, but for now we just don't know how we are going to make it."

The rest of the train ride was quiet. Everyone was lost in thought. Some were glad they didn't have to face what this family was facing. Some had lost a loved one and knew the difficult road ahead. All of them were changed. Their perspective went from one of annoyance to one of love and empathy for this father and his children in the blink of an eye.

You don't know what someone is dealing with until you have walked in that person's shoes. Maybe the person bullying you just needs to be understood and shown a caring heart. You could change that person's life and make a difference. All it takes is some understanding on your part and some education on the bully's.

Refresher of what you have learned:

You can overcome fear.

You can educate yourself and others.

You can replace old programming with new, improved thinking.

You choose what you believe.

You can make a difference.

What you want to remember:

6

I LOVE YOU

"Our mind can be our best friend or our worst enemy depending on what we choose to do with it."
— *Carol Tuttle*

Scientists have discovered that all life is connected. You cannot hurt someone else without hurting yourself. You cannot help someone without helping yourself. We are all connected. The Law of Sensitive Dependence upon Initial Conditions, also known as the butterfly effect, was proven in the 1990s. It started in 1963 when Edward Lorenz presented a hypothesis to the New York Academy of Science. He stated that a butterfly could flap its wings, and that would move molecules of air that would eventually build until it became a hurricane on the other side of the planet.

You can look back through history to see how one person made a move that still affects us today. Colonel Chamberlain of the Union Army in Gettysburg, Norman Borlaug, Henry Wallace, George Washington Carver, and Moses and Susan Carver are all great examples of the butterfly effect. When you face a person who gives you the opportunity to grow and become better equipped, remember that both of you are connected in some way. If you look at a bully as someone who is dealing with problems just as you are, you realize the chance to show maturity and thoughtfulness. You have the ability to rise above the pain and help a person in need. When we help one another, we make the world better.

When we show love and respect for our fellow man, we leave the world a better place. You can respect someone as a person even if you don't respect the person's beliefs or actions. Life is precious. Respect means a relation to something or high or special regard. You can respect life without respecting behavior. When someone you love misbehaves or makes a bad decision, you still love and respect them, you just don't agree with the behavior or choices. You can separate the two. You can treat a bully with respect and still stand up for yourself and others. Think about how you want your loved ones or family members treated when they make a mistake.

Bullies are family members also. They have mothers and fathers. They might even have brothers and sisters, aunts and uncles. Their grandparents love them just like yours love you. When you remember the bully is in pain and lashing out, it is much easier to choose the higher road and walk away. Then you can turn to your family and friends to get the support and love you need. The bully may not have that. You have an enormous support group that you can utilize to build your self-esteem back up. You can say, "Thank you for your opinion" and move on.

I have a beautiful example involving a former student of mine. Her name is Tawnie McIntire. She was recently called the *B* word. She thought about how that word means a female dog. Dogs bark. Bark is on trees. Trees are beautiful and provide us with many wonderful things. She told the bully, "Thank you." The bully looked at her in wonder and left her alone. That is the perfect example of what I am discussing.

You choose the impact of others' words and how they affect your moment, day, or life. In my three-day trainings, I have participants let go of baggage they have been holding onto for years, some of them for thirty or forty years. You don't have to do that. You can make a choice right now to live your life on your terms and by your standards. Charles Swindoll, author and educator, says, "I am convinced that life is 10 percent what happens to me and 90 percent how I react to it." I have found that to be true in my life. You don't have to relive pain and trauma. You can ease your pain by making a different decision.

You can choose to love and respect all life. You can choose to help others ease their pain. You can choose to be nice no matter what. If you slip and lash out at someone, as we all do because we are human after all, ask forgiveness. If the person chooses not to give it to you, it doesn't really matter because you are asking for yourself and your health. Whatever you do, don't hold it inside to poison your body slowly. You also need to forgive yourself. I still have reminders on my wall to make sure I do this on a daily basis. The golden rule applies to you and the way you treat yourself as well.

There are many versions of the golden rule: do unto others as you would have them do unto you. What it means to me is that I need to treat you how I want to be treated. I also need to treat myself the same way. I need to love and respect all life, even my own. When someone says things to you that is not so nice, or treats you with a lack of integrity, you decide whether to follow the golden rule or lower yourself to their level. You'll make this decision many times in your life, and sometimes many times in one day. Each time you make the right decision, it gets easier to make again and again. I believe that if I choose to be nice, my rewards will be great, and my belief has been proven time and again in my life and in the lives of my children and my husband. We are blessed in many ways. I am grateful for all the Lord has given to me, and I know it is because of my choice to follow him. His life was filled with example after example of how the golden rule should be lived and applied. Nelson Mandela's life is another example of how we should treat others. You can also look to Mahatma Gandhi if you need further proof.

When you show tolerance to others, tolerance is shown to you. That which you give out, you get back. This is the natural law of the harvest that we already discussed: you reap what you sow. If you plant corn seeds, you will never eat watermelons. You have to plant watermelon seeds in order to eat watermelons. The same is true with life. If you want kindness shown to you,

you must show kindness to others. If you want to be forgiven, you must forgive others. If you want to be blessed, you must bless others. Truth, love, happiness, integrity, and kindness are the simple things in life that make all the difference in your living of it. The items you receive for free are the most important. People often place little value on the free things; however, they are the most valuable. They are the foundation on which all else is built. The first thing you received was your life. Have you thanked your parents lately? They may not have raised you the way you would have liked, but they did raise you to the best of their abilities. They gave you the precious gift of life and all that comes with it. Think of all the enjoyable things you experienced just because you live. That is something to be grateful for, so show some gratitude.

Make a list of 100 things you're grateful for. (wb) No repeating. Don't go on until you do this. Now that you are in a grateful mood, think of others who have not made the decision to be grateful. Now that you are grateful, your perspective has likely changed. You may feel lighter, happier, and maybe even stronger. I do when I'm grateful. Show some compassion to those who have not made the choice to love and respect others. Be an example of what it is like to live your life with gratitude and love for your fellow man. How would you feel if someone smiled at you—a real, heartwarming smile—when you were having a bad day?

When I was in college, I came across a little book called *PS I Love You*. It was a compilation of notes H. Jackson Brown Jr.'s, inspirational author, mother had given him in his lunchbox. The notes where short and printed on postcards you could mail to loved ones. I tore those cards out and hung them on my wall as physical reminders to keep me moving toward my goal. One of them was, "Give a stranger one of your beautiful smiles. It may be the only sunshine he sees all day." I took it to heart and started doing it. The reactions I get are amazing. Try it and see what happens. (wb) How amazing is it to change a life with a smile? It feels great!

I started this book by stating that we are all different, incredible beings. I'll now tell you how we are the same. Everyone has the same wishes and needs you do. They love their families and are doing the best they can with what they have. They bleed when they are cut, and they have the ability to heal. They need to be loved and respected. They need to be heard and listened to. They need someone to care when they are feeling down. It makes sense that if you are the same, in some respects, as they are, that you could love and care for them.

If you are having a hard time with the idea that everyone is the same, think of symbiosis. Symbiosis is when two dissimilar organisms live together in a mutually beneficial relationship, like you and your pets. Many people have pets that they would choose to not live without. Some people think of their pets as family. Regardless of how you feel about pets, they are examples of dissimilar life forces living in harmony. You can find your own example if this one doesn't work for you. You can choose to have a symbiotic relationship with others. Think of how much better this world would be if we could all get along. I don't mean become like one another. I mean get along. There would be no need to change anyone else. There would be no need to have a "protected class." All life would be respected for what it was. Hunters and animal rights people could talk to one another in a civil manner. No religion would be better than the others. You wouldn't have bigotry or prejudice. People would live together while living their own lives, everyone going about their business, never hurting one another, just living their lives to the best of their abilities.

When I was younger, I paid a friend of mine to not go hunting. Later that month I was out to lunch with another one of my friends, whom I'll call Lisa. I ordered a steak, and Lisa said, "I thought you didn't eat meat."

I said, "I was raised a vegetarian, but I am not anymore."

She said, "But I heard you paid John to not go hunting."

"I did," I said.

She looked confused. I went on to explain my reasoning. The cow I was eating was already dead and there was nothing I could do about it. However, the other animal was still alive. I could save a deer's life with my action in that time and place. I chose to make a difference in a way I felt I could. Death is a part of life. If you are living, you will die. I have some control over when I will die. I exercise, eat healthy food, wear my seatbelt, and don't smoke or do illegal drugs. These choices help me live a longer, healthier life, but they won't help me live forever.

My dad used to say, "You're not getting out of this life alive." He was right. We will all transition someday and, when we do, life here on earth still goes on. You need to enjoy life and allow others to enjoy theirs while you are here.

Just as you have your rights, others have theirs. Our society seems to have forgotten that your rights end where my nose begins. You have the right to live your life as you see fit. I also have that right. America was founded on individual rights, freedoms, and liberties for all people. However, with rights come responsibilities, and both are equally important. You are responsible for your choices and the consequences they cause. Think about the consequences before you make the decision and act. When one person misbehaves, this does not mean that you can. You still have the responsibility to think and act responsibly. Two negatives make a positive only in mathematics and nowhere else. A driver education student once told me that three lefts make a right. I answered that it's easier just to make the right in the first place. The same is true here. You need to do it right the first time. Be responsible for your rights and the rights of others.

I know that Hollywood is saying something else. Movies come out that depict the message that it is all right to hurt others if they hurt you first. This is not true. Violence begets violence, which leads to more violence, and it continues to grow and escalate. Be the one to stop the violence. Take responsibility for your actions and stop trying to blame someone else's behavior for your decisions. It's hard to do at times, but if we are to end the pain and suffering caused by violence, we must do it.

Elizabeth Smart's case is a good example of how people who have wronged you should be dealt with. She is an incredibly strong and smart woman. She did what she had to do to protect those she loved and to survive. Then she made sure that Brian David Mitchell was brought to justice so he couldn't hurt others. Those are the kind of movies society should produce and headline. There are some good movies that I believe you should watch, and I have listed some of them in the back of this book.

There are a few groups of people who think competition is one of the reasons for bullying. I disagree with them. Competition is good. Like anything else, it can be carried to an extreme, but it teaches some valuable lessons. Competition is when you strive to win. When you have the desire to be the best you can be, you work harder, more efficiently, and smarter, and you do your best. We are not created equal in the sense that we are all the same. We are all valuable, we all have talents, and no one is better than anyone else. However, we are not equal. My son, Max, is six-foot-seven and he just turned fifteen. His life is different from the lives of his friends who are five-five. Not better, just different. I am six feet tall, and I was by the time I was fifteen. I had different experiences because of my height. Not better, not worse, just different. Height is one of the things you cannot change about yourself. Whether growing is a competition depends on your perspective. Height is an advantage in basketball, Max loves basketball, so he does all he can to grow as tall as possible. If you eat healthy foods, get plenty of rest, drink water, stay away from illegal drugs, and take care of yourself, you have a better chance of reaching the height you were meant to be. You have to do what you can do to be the best you can be. When there is no competition, you can slack off. You don't have to give it your best effort because it doesn't matter. There is no best. There is nothing to push you to be better than you currently are because there is no reason.

Competition between teams or individuals can create a close bond. My experience as a basketball player, coach, and member of the military has taught me that there is no closer bond then the one I can build with my team members. I had the privilege of making the University of Utah Ranger Challenge team. I was the first female to do so, and it took me two years of intense training. I know that if I needed help from any of the members of the team, I could contact them and they would come. I haven't spoken with them for years, but I know that all I would have to do is ask. The same is true for my fellow basketball players. That is the type of bonds you develop while you push yourself hard every day to get better. When you are forged in fire, your bond is tighter. You are welded together as a united team. We need to allow more competition. Society needs to foster the mentality that each member must be the best they can be so our country is the best it can be.

We all need to do the best we can. We need to strive to continually grow in all areas of life: physical, mental, emotional, spiritual, and financial. Remember when I talked about taking care of your own front lawn so the neighborhood would be a better place? I cannot be the best I can be if I keep focusing on your faults. Energy flows where attention goes. What that means is that the more you think about something, the bigger it gets. When you focus on being the best you can be, you get better. Live your life and let those around you live theirs. It is not your place to say how they should live it. It is not your place to make them like you. You were created unique for a reason. It would be boring if everyone was exactly alike. Think about it for a moment. A bunch of *you*s walking around. Talk about competition. What if they made the same decisions you made at the same time you did? It gives rush-hour traffic an entirely new meaning. You may think you want everyone to believe the same things you do and to like the same things you do but, in reality, you don't. Maybe you feel unsure or confused by their choices. You don't have to be. When you come from a place of love for others, you can let them be themselves with no hard feelings. You don't have to get upset or attack them. You just love them. Live and let live.

There is a time for everything: a time to be quiet, a time to talk, a time to stand up, a time to sit down, a time to cry, a time to laugh, a time to challenge yourself, and a time to just let be. Now is the time to choose how you will live your life. Now is the time to become a better you. Now is the time to be an example to those around you. Show respect and love to others. Be grateful for the many abilities and talents you have. Feel blessed. Now is the time to change.

Recap of the chapter concepts:

All life is connected.

Every person is loved.

You can ease another's pain.

You decide how the movie ends.

Competition pushes you to be better.

Live and let live.

There is a time for everything.

What you want to remember:

PLANNED RESPONSES

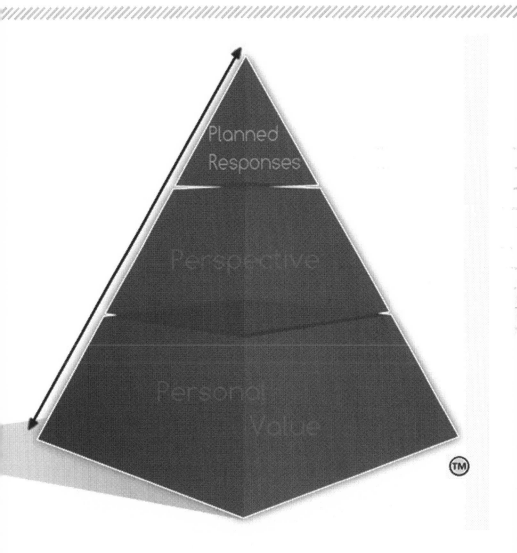

7

SPIDERS, SNAKES, AND PUBLIC SPEAKING

"Man's mind is his basic tool of survival. Life is given to him, survival is not...His mind is given to him, its content is not...to remain alive, he must think."
— Ayn Rand

A phobia is the irrational, persistent fear of something. There are some 530 phobias listed at phobialist.com. Some you probably think are silly, and others you agree with. If you are the person with arachibutyrophobia, the fear of peanut butter sticking to the roof of your mouth, it can be scary for you. A phobia is an irrational, persistent fear that you can do something about with the proper help. I don't want to cure you of your phobias. In fact, I want to use them to help you practice bully proofing yourself. When you are bullied, your heart rate goes up, your breathing gets faster, your palms might start to sweat, and you can't think very well. The "can't think very well," is the one we'll focus on.

Think about where the fear comes from when you are being bullied. Most likely, it comes from the fear of possible future pain, either from humiliation or from abuse. When you have a fear-based reaction, you enter what is referred to as the freeze, fight, or flight sympathetic nervous system response. You have no control over the physiological reaction; however, you do have control over your response to the cause. Let me explain by telling you a story.

When I was a young girl growing up on our farm in Washington state, my brother and I had to fill the inside wood box. It wasn't a difficult task, but it was always nice to have two people performing this particular chore. One of us would get the wood from the woodpile outside, while the other stood at the back door, waiting to bring it the rest of the way into the house. This way we didn't have to take our shoes off to come in, and the task was completed more efficiently. My brother was always a gentleman and let me remain inside because I don't like the cold. He also enjoyed making me jump.

We entered the back door of our house through the garage. There was a bathroom door as we stepped into the mud room—it was Washington, after all, and we did live on a farm. Sometimes he liked to step into the bathroom after he handed me the wood. I would drop the wood off in the box and return for more. He would step out of the bathroom door and say, "Boo!" He liked my reaction. Once I jumped so high that I landed on my back and hit my head. He stopped after that. He didn't want to hurt me. He just liked to hear me scream and see my hair stand on end and my eyes get as big a dinner plates. It was all in fun and it kept my nervous system in top shape.

Flash forward about six years to 1986. I was at Fort Dix, New Jersey, in army basic training. I was walking down the hall in our barracks when Drill Sergeant Young stepped into the doorway. You guessed it: I reacted the way I had been trained. My hair shot up, my eyes got big, and I screamed…to which he replied, "This will never do, Private."

He spent the next six weeks training me to a new reaction pattern. That was fun. No, really, it was. I could hardly wait to get home and fill the wood box with Robbie.

Flash forward another seven years to 1993 and my teaching job. I was still a new teacher, having only been teaching for two years. I had just started my career at Summit High School. I was in my classroom, grading papers. It was quiet and I thought everyone had gone home. I got up from my desk to go to the restroom. I opened my door and a student was standing there. Once again, I reacted. As I looked at the student lying on the floor, I knew my teaching career was over. I went directly to our counselor at the time and told him what I had done. We returned to my classroom to find the student sitting in a desk. I asked him if he was all right and apologized. The counselor asked him if he wanted to press charges.

"No way, man, it will ruin my rep." There are so many benefits to working with gang members; I just never knew this would be one. Can you imagine the backlash he would have received? "You got beat up by your teacher? A female teacher?" We never spoke of the incident again.

My career went forward, and he was a well-behaved student. When other students got mouthy, he would step up and say, "You need to sit down and leave her alone." He was my protector for many years. Students talked about how I was his favorite teacher and you better not mess with me or you had to answer to him. He was one of my favorites too.

I have since changed my reaction once again. However, I still recommend making noise as you approach. It might make the meeting better for both of us.

I tell this story to illustrate the point that you can choose your reaction and practice it until it becomes habit. You can choose how you will react when you are scared. First you have to decide how you want to react. You'll need different reactions for different situations. Fear is not always bad. It can keep you alive. I don't play in the street because I like being round and am afraid of ending up flat. I don't jump off buildings because I'm afraid of the sudden stop at the end. Please keep some of your fears; I'm just talking about the ones you want to change to make your life better.

Ask yourself where the fear is coming from. Consider whether the fear is something you need to keep you alive, or if you need to act in spite of it. Courage is not the absence of fear, it is the action taken to move through the fear. If there is no fear, there is no courage. Courage is acting in spite of fear. It is answering the question "What if…" and then taking the best course of action. Napoleon Bonaparte and Andrew Jackson have been quoted as saying, "Take time to deliberate, but when the time for action has arrived, stop thinking and go in."

When considering something new or different, assess the situation. Ask yourself, "What if…?" and then answer with all the positive and negative things you can think of. If you have time, ask others for their input. Ask people who have done what you are trying to do. They will have insight that is pertinent to the situation. Notice I said *the* situation, and not necessarily *your* situation. Now you have to decide what action you will take.

I believe that every person on this planet was put here with a purpose to fulfill. I have no idea what your purpose is. I only know what mine is, and that is to teach. I love to learn and I love to pass that knowledge on. When I was in high school, I decided to be a teacher and help others, just like Pat Emerson helped me. There were others who helped me press on toward the mark. My parents were powerful forces behind me. They spent time and money getting me the medical help and specialists that would help me live and grow. They always told me I could do it. For many years, I didn't see it. I thought I was worthless. I let the words of mean people define who I was, the naysayers who said, "You will never make it. You're too stupid." I want to thank those who have helped me move forward in spite of my fears by helping others do the same. Some people took me by the hand and lead me through the rough patches. Some inspired me with words of, "You will never make it." When I hear words like, "You can't do it," "You're not smart enough," "You're so stupid you can't even read," my back hair goes up. I take the bit in my mouth and run with it. It may not always be pretty, but I get it done. When you find yourself feeling down or unsure, look up at all the people standing there with their hands outstretched, reaching back to help you.

You need to learn how to act in spite of fear. Start with some of your smaller phobias. Think of how they control you and limit you in some way. Perhaps you are missing out on some aspect of life because of your fear, or you are not living to your full potential because of it. You could be living a fuller, more rewarding life. You could have more fun with your family and enjoy your time with them. If so, it is time to take action. Remember the exercise you did at the beginning of the book regarding your comfort zone? It's time to pull it out and look at it. Pick one thing that is outside your comfort zone that you want to bring in. Now answer the question "Why?" Why do you want to be a person who has this skill or ability? How would your life change if you could do it? Set a timer for five minutes and write it down. (wb) Cover all the senses: what your new life would look like with this new ability, what you would hear that you haven't heard before, new smells you would experience, new foods you might eat, new things you would touch and experience and, most importantly, how you would feel emotionally.

When you get this kind of detail on why you want to change, the change is made easier. You get excited to experience all these new things and you are pulled into your future instead of pushed. When you are pulled, someone or something is helping you and giving you that extra lift you need to make it to the next step. When you try to push yourself, you resist because you feel it is against your will. Let your vision pull you forward. Expand your comfort zone to include new and exciting things. Stop standing on the sidelines when you want to be in the game. It doesn't matter how you play, just do the best you can with what you have at the time. My dad always said, "Be the best you can be. Not the best, just the best you can be." I am so grateful for those words. They pulled me forward when I didn't have the strength. They helped me do something just one more time.

Steve Brown, radio broadcaster and author, wrote, "Anything worth doing is worth doing poorly—until you learn to do it well." The first time I read that, I thought I knew what it said. Then I stopped myself and read it slowly about five times. I let it sink in and thought about the things I wasn't doing because I wanted to be perfect at them. My world opened up even more. Stop worrying what others will say about you and start living. Drink deeply from your life well. Use every speck of life you have to live. Stretch, grow, learn new things, enjoy what you have, and be grateful. Once you stretch your comfort zone, it will never go back to its original shape, and the more you stretch it, the easier it gets. Stop letting fears hold you back. Go live your life.

When you overcome limiting beliefs or fears, your self-confidence grows. Self-confidence is earned, not given. You earn it when you do something you didn't think you could. It grows when you perform a difficult task. The more you overcome, the more likely you are to continue overcoming difficulties in your life. You become a problem solver and a solution finder who can help others. To keep me moving forward, I tell myself, "Check your safety gear. Make sure it is in good working order. Review protocol. Hold your mask and regulator. Jump in with both feet."

For a long time, I let a fear of water hold me back from enjoying warm weather activities. One of my favorite trips was to Hawaii when my entire family went scuba diving. If I had not overcome my fear of the water, we wouldn't have had as much fun. Max, our youngest son, earned his junior scuba certification when he was ten, just a few months before we left. Underwater is a different world. It was exciting to watch Laurence, Erin, and Max discover new things, and I was right there with them, not sitting on the shore. It still takes a great deal of courage for me to get into the water, but it is always worth it. We are planning another trip to Australia to dive the Great Barrier Reef when Max graduates from high school.

When I want to shrink back from something, I remember the scuba lessons and the trip to Hawaii. Check your safety gear and jump in with both feet.

When you learn how to overcome your fears, the world is your playground. You have no limits. You have a newfound freedom. You don't know why you waited so long to create this new you. You wonder where else you are holding yourself back. You'll find and remove the blocks that keep you stuck. You allow yourself to experience things you only dreamed of before. You find a new strength and power that lets you stand tall. When you stand in your power, others can't hurt you. They can't take advantage of you or put you down.

Eleanor Roosevelt said, "People cannot make you feel inferior without your permission." You need to face your fear and stand in your power when people say things about you that you don't like. You can choose how you respond. When you know you are valuable, you don't have to try and prove it. When you understand the value of each person, you don't try to diminish it, you let it shine. When I present this concept in my trainings, I tell people that whatever they focus on gets bigger. "Energy flows where attention goes." Motivational speaker James Ray taught me that.

If I focus on the bad in my life, it gets worse. If I keep reliving a moment of sadness or anxiety, my sadness and anxiety gets deeper. The young girl in Florida who committed suicide because of cyberbullying, Rebecca Sedwick, was bullied using social media. She spent time thinking about it. She kept going over it in her mind. She fed it energy and then she made the decision that the only way to stop it was to end her life. This is a tragic example of what can happen when focus is placed on the wrong things. My heart and prayers are with her family. She could have survived if she had placed her energy on uplifting things.

I think of Elizabeth Smart and what she went through. Talk about an extreme case of bullying. When she returned home, her mother gave her the best possible advice. Elizabeth took it to heart and says it changed her life. Lois Smart said (Smart 2013, 285-286):

> *Elizabeth, what this man has done is terrible. There aren't*
> *any words strong enough to describe how wicked and evil he*

is! He has taken nine months of your life that you will never get back again. But the best punishment you could ever give him is to be happy. To move forward with your life. To do exactly what you want. Because, yes, this will probably go to trial and some kind of sentencing will be given to him and that wicked woman. But even if that's true, you may never feel like justice has been served or that true restitution has been made. But you don't need to worry about that. At the end of the day, God is our ultimate judge. He will make up to you every pain and loss that you have suffered. And if it turns out that these wicked people are not punished here on earth, it doesn't matter. His punishments are just. You don't have to worry. You don't ever have to even think about them again. You be happy, Elizabeth. Just be happy. If you go and feel sorry for yourself, or if you dwell on what has happened, if you hold on to your pain, that is allowing him to steal more of your life away. So don't you do that! Don't you let him! There is no way he deserves that. Not one more second of your life. You keep every second for yourself. You keep them and be happy. God will take care of the rest.

Make the decision to be happy. Decide to live your life to its fullest in spite of all the bad things out there. You can control your reactions to what happens to you. You are the captain of your fate and the master of your soul. To get something you've never had, you must do something you've never done. Try living your life instead of shrinking back in fear; you might just like it.

Recap of what you were presented:

You can choose your reaction when presented with a stimulus.

You give energy to the things you focus on, which makes them bigger.

You can design your reactions to outside stimuli.

You decide how others will impact you.

You can overcome fear.

What you want to remember:

8

STRETCH YOUR COMFORT ZONE

"You must decide what you choose to create and what you are willing to do to create it."
— James Arthur Ray

Get out the comfort zone exercise you did in chapter one. Your comfort zone contains all the things you're comfortable with. Were there any surprises, or anything you wanted to add or get rid of? That is what this chapter is about—making changes to your comfort zone.

You may wonder why you should stretch your comfort zone. Stretching your comfort zone will change your life in profound ways and transform you in ways you never thought possible. You will discover new worlds and new people. You will build your self-confidence and learn to be more tolerant of others and their ways of life. You will expand your mind and learn more about yourself and why you do the things you do. You will create new dimensions to your personality and character. When you stretch your comfort zone, you will have new experiences and become a better problem solver.

Your comfort zone represents everything you have in your life. You enjoy and get a reward from these things. You may complain about some of them, but you still have them. To get something you've never had, you must do something you've never done. To get something you want, you must do something new. In other words, you must stretch your comfort zone. You must change some things about yourself and what you're doing. Why? So you can have new things, new experiences, new perspectives, and a new life. It doesn't have to be so new that you don't recognize it. It can be the same life, only better.

Sometimes when I bring this idea up in my trainings, people start looking for the exits. Why does change scare people so much? It's a part of life. If things didn't change, you'd still be sucking your thumb and sitting in your own mess. If time stood still like you wished it did while you were on your perfect date in the tenth grade, you wouldn't be sitting with the love of your life with your kids down the hall. You might forget how beautiful fall is and how excited you get when the snow melts and the buds start to grow. You wouldn't get to live each day to its fullest. That trip down memory lane wouldn't be very long if the world had stopped because you were in pain. Be thankful for change and embrace it; use it to improve yourself.

Think of something difficult you've done—something you really struggled with and had no idea how to make it happen. Now remind yourself how good it felt when you accomplished it. You probably celebrated by doing the Snoopy dance and told everyone you had made it. If you didn't, do it now. Feel pride in your accomplishments. Let it fill you from the bottom of your feet to the top of your head. Revel in your ability to overcome obstacles, in the power of your mind to break down barriers that held you back or tried to stop you. Let your self-confidence grow. Let yourself feel amazing, because you are. Realize that when you did that tough thing, you stretched your comfort zone. (wb)

Each time you step forward through pain or hardship, you get stronger and smarter. You build your personal value and stretch your comfort zone to a new size. You allow yourself to have new experiences. You may have missed out on things because you were afraid or thought you couldn't do them. Go watch the Special Olympics or spend time with a child who has lost a limb and now plays sports. There are examples of people who could have used excuses to hold themselves back, but who are living the life they dreamed of because they just did it. They wouldn't take "no" or "you can't do that" for an answer. They went out and made their own truths, and you can too.

Stop sitting on the sidelines and go play the game. If there's music, dance. If there's water, splash. If there's a ball, hit it, shoot it, throw it, bounce it, kick it. Let your body know it's alive. If you're in chronic pain, you might as well have fun because you'll still hurt anyway. If the pain needs to heal, let it heal with gratitude in your heart for the things you can still do. Play in the PlayPlace at McDonald's. Throw that snowball, make the snow angels, and then go drink hot chocolate by the fire. Do the things you love. Ask others what they like, and try that as well. Love yourself and those you're with. Laugh at yourself and the funny things people do. Live your life. Life is not for spectators; life is for playing.

As you stretch, you grow and learn more about yourself and others. The more life experiences you have, the more understanding you have.

I think it's funny when someone asks me how something tastes. How do you explain watermelon or a fresh strawberry? How do you explain the sunset from the Wal-Mart in Hawaii? One of the best ones I've ever seen. How do you reproduce the sound of a mother moose while she is talking to her calf? You can't. It's just not the same. If you want to know what something looks like, smells like, tastes like, feels like, or sounds like, go experience it for yourself. Your experience will be different from mine or anyone else's. If you have the desire, you have the ability to make it so. If you have lost the desire, rekindle it. Find the passion that you lost; dig up that urge you once had. Remember what you once wished for.

My husband gave my dreams back to me. I lost them while trying to support myself and my daughter. While trying to make it to the next day, I got bogged down with life and not living. He taught me to stop, lift my head up, and enjoy the beauty that is all around. Then he taught me to dream and wish for more. He helped teach me to have the courage to face my fears and make it happen. He reminded me that anything is possible.

Blair Singer, Rich Dad advisor and educator, taught me to stop trying to improve my weaknesses and to strengthen my strengths instead. He says that to be the best, you have to work at being the best. Stop wasting time on what you're not talented at, and do what you are good at. If Tiger Woods had worked on his jump shot, we wouldn't know who he was. Tiger was not meant to be a basketball player. He is made to play golf, and this is why he is so good at golf. He took his talent and made it better. Michael Jordan was not meant to play baseball, but give him a basketball and be amazed. The man is poetry in motion. Thank goodness he worked so hard at being better and making his high school basketball team. Think of all we would have missed if he had given up. What if your talent is just outside your comfort zone, and you never find it because you are afraid? You could be the next Adele or J.K. Rowling don't let a little fear stand in your way.

Stretching your comfort zone will also broaden your perspective. You'll see things in a different way. When I was going to college and money was tight, when I didn't even have the money to buy Erin a ten-cent treat, I was always able to find someone who had it worse than me. I would use that person as an example that things could get worse. When I drove around town and saw the homeless people, a wave of gratitude washed over me. I was so glad I was not living on the street with my little girl.

When things were going great and everything was fine, I sometimes drove by the capitol and looked at all the incredible homes. I pictured Erin coming out the front door on her way to someplace nice. She would have clothes that fit and that didn't have holes in them. She would get into her car with her friends and go out to dinner. I have that now, because I was willing to get back to work and school. I was willing to do what it took to make my dreams come true. I'm still dreaming and working, and I love every minute of it. I wouldn't change a thing. I am proud that Erin never went to bed hungry. She always had food, shelter, and plenty of love.

If I had not done what I did when I did it, we wouldn't be where we are now. My life was not the life I planned as a little girl lying in the grass watching the clouds drift by, but it's getting close. If I had not had the courage to stretch my comfort zone, I wouldn't be where I am today. I definitely wouldn't be writing a book and speaking from a stage.

When you have new experiences, you find you are more tolerant of others and their ways of life. You may not agree with what they do, but as long as they aren't hurting you or your loved ones, you can live and let them live the way they want to. Just as you can't describe the sweet taste of a strawberry you've never eaten, you can't understand someone else's pain if you've never lived through any of your own. If you've never moved through your fears, you don't understand the single mother facing hers. If you've never tried something new, you can't help your children when they want to spread their wings and fly. When my son, Max, was two, I was a single parent again. My mom took the three of us, Erin, Max, and I, to Idaho where she had grown up, and she enjoyed going back in the summer. I loved to go to hotels and jump on the beds. No one is there to tell you not to. It's so much fun, I still do it sometimes. Try it. I also go outside in my socks. Don't tell my mom though.

Back to the trip to Idaho. We stopped at a diner for lunch. I think we were the only ones in the place, which was nice as Max could be a little hyper after riding in the car for a while. He was jumping back and forth from one booth to the other, and I let him. After about six or seven times, he stood up on the booth and asked, "Mom, when are you going to teach me how to fly?"

Our waitress had just walked up, and she said, "Yeah, Mom, when?"

I told him, "Max, I can't teach you something I don't know how to do. As soon as I learn how, you'll be the first one I teach." You can't teach what you don't know, and you can't tolerate what you don't understand. Try something new, and expand your tolerance for others.

An expanded comfort zone deepens your character. It adds dimensions and angles to your personality that weren't there before. Think of a crystal or a diamond. The more facets it has, the more it sparkles. I have a beautiful Celtic crystal that my mother-in-law brought us from Ireland that sits in the window of my office. When the sun hits it, I am blessed with the most incredible rainbow room. I sit back in my chair and feel the gratitude of where I am. If that crystal didn't have so many facets, it wouldn't make as many rainbows. The same is true with you. If you just keep doing what you've always done, you can get a little flat and boring.

How do you stretch your comfort zone? Pick something you've wanted to do, and do it. Educate yourself first if it's skydiving—you don't want to just go jump out of a plane. I think you need one of those parachute things. Then check your safety gear, and jump.

If you're thinking of talking to someone cute across the room, jump in and do it. No safety gear required. Get up, walk over, and say, "Hi." You can even talk to your shoes if it feels better. It's a start and, at this point in the game, that's what you're looking for: forward momentum that can carry into the next wonderful experience. After you say hi, that person may become your best friend or may slap your face, depending on what you say next. I can't tell you what to say next, because it depends on you and the circumstances. Take a chance and expand your comfort zone. Keep doing it until you get the results you want. Measure, monitor, and adjust until it equals the results you desire. If you don't light the match, you can't light the candle.

That's all there is to it. Think of something and then go do it. The more you stretch, the easier it is to stretch. Every time you shrink back in fear, the easier it becomes to shrink. You may have to overcome some shrinkage at first, but keep it up. It's like a muscle—the more you work it and stretch it, the stronger and more flexible it becomes.

Your comfort zone may be like a rubber band that has been in the freezer for a long time. Start with some small stretches, and build up to the bigger stuff. Get it warmed up with little pulls, and work up to the big ones. If you take a rubber band out of the freezer and pull on it, it will break. I don't think you can break your comfort zone, but it is easier to start small and grow.

I'm not sure I would have just gone out and jumped into the ocean in Hawaii. I took little steps, starting at the shallow end of the pool and moving into the deep. After that, we went up to "the Crater" at the Homestead Resort. Because of all the little steps, I was able to make it to the dive in Hawaii. I still dive once a year just to keep the safety procedures fresh in my mind and the fear at bay. Max usually goes with me. He is such a fish and so relaxed that it helps me.

After Max's dad and I divorced, I was doing sweat equity on a home for us out in Eagle Mountain. I was honor-bound to do the roofing because I said I would. I had a crew of friends that said they would come help me. On the day I was to shingle the roof, no one showed up. I didn't know how I would get it done. My neighbor helped me tie some ropes together so I could tie off and not kill myself. The visions that ran through my mind that morning. He could only stay for a few hours, but it got me going. At about ten o'clock, I was on the roof and a gentleman asked from behind me where my crew was. I didn't turn around because I was afraid to move too fast, but I answered, "You're looking at it."

"That's just not right," he said. He left and in about ten minutes he came back with two other men. They got to work and I handed out shingles. I watched in amazement as they completed my roof. They ran around with no ropes or fear.

I felt silly with all my tie-down gear. I asked him if he ever tied off.

He answered, "Only on a twelve-pitch."

I said, "What's this?"

"A ten."

"Oh. Could I die if I fall off?"

"No, but you might sprain something."

I could live with a sprain, so I took my safety gear off and, by the end of the day, I was doing all right. I wasn't as at ease as he was, but he did this for a living. But I was moving around on my feet and not crawling any more. When the roof was done, I asked him what I owed him.

"Nothing. Glad I could help."

He did, in many ways. His confidence helped build mine. I stretched during the building of that home and was proud of it. It was perfect for the three of us, and I had done that. Pretty cool. Now my husband and I own rental homes. My favorite part of rehabbing our rentals is the demolition phase. However, when we had to roof the garage at Twenty-Ninth Street, I was up there with Laurence. A comfort zone, once stretched, does not return to its original state.

Pick something today and do it. The longer you wait, the harder it gets, and pretty soon you're right back were you were. Do it now. Stretch yourself.

Before when I discussed comfort zones, I told you I wouldn't make any judgment calls. Well, now I am. You know what you should be doing. Make it so. Pick something and do it. If you need to stop smoking, then stop. The effects cigarettes have on you are easy to forget because they're not in your face every day. What if they were? Sometimes you know the right thing to do, but you don't always do it, and someone else may pay the price. Do you want to live with that?

When I was ten months old, I had a problem. Whenever my mom laid me down, I cried and turned blue. Her intuition told her something was wrong. The doctor thought I was spoiled, but he ordered an X-ray to be sure. My mom said he came out as white as a ghost. I had a tumor in my chest that restricted my breathing whenever she laid me down.

They cut me from my sternum to my spine—yup, I've been cut in half—and took out three inches from three of my ribs. I had malignant mesenchymosarcoma, a cancerous growth in my chest. It is an extremely rare form of cancer, and Doctor Schabacker said my medical records would travel all over the world so that others could learn from them.

I never really thought about it growing up. It was just the way it was. I have pretty bad scoliosis because of it, and I was told by another doctor that if it weren't for the scoliosis, I would be six-foot-two.

When I came back from Fort Dix, New Jersey and basic training, I told my dad it was hard to breathe sometimes. I noticed it during basketball, but nothing like the training I received from Drill Sergeant Young. My dad looked me in the eye and said, "I'm sorry about that." It got me thinking. My dad smoked when I was young and while my mom was pregnant with me. Did he cause my cancer? No one knows, but I know my dad beat himself up over it for years. I know he felt responsible in some way. I know because I am a parent, and you always wonder if you're doing it right. When Erin was diagnosed with some learning differences, I blamed myself and that tiny sip of champagne I had on New Year's Eve. As a parent, you do the best you can with what you know at the time. That's all you can do. The good thing about kids is that they're pretty tough and the mistakes we make can be learning experiences for them.

I never blamed my dad for anything in my life, but I sure do give him credit for helping me become the wonderful parent I am. I know I've made mistakes and I learned from them and became stronger. I hope he doesn't blame himself. I know a parent who did.

On October 26, 2000, Paul Wayment found out what it was like to live with a bad decision. This story still makes me cry because Gage was two, the same age as Max. Paul wanted to scout deer for the hunt, and he took Gage with him. Gage fell asleep in the truck, and Paul locked the doors and went out scouting anyway. When he came back, Gage was missing. Hundreds of people searched. The ex-wife was blamed. Paul was blamed. Strangers were blamed. I remember feeling the dread in my gut. Every time I looked at Max, a knot twisted in my stomach. Max's dad and I argued about it. We were going through a divorce at the time. He blamed the mother, and I said that Paul had made a horrible mistake.

They found Gage a few days later. He had frozen to death. They believe Gage woke up and went in search of his dad. I can't imagine trying to live with that kind of a mistake. Paul couldn't. He committed suicide in the spot where his son had died. I believe that as Paul locked that door, he thought everything would be all right. Nothing could go wrong. He'd only be gone a short while. I believe that because we all have a voice inside us telling us what to do. The problem is knowing when to listen and when to tell it to shut up. I also learned that when I hear it, I need to pay attention and double check my safety gear.

I'm in no way saying I'm better then Paul or that he was stupid. I only feel sorrow for the family, and I learned a lesson from their loss. I hope you do too. Think about what you're doing at all times. Think about the worst, and best, possible outcomes you might face while stretching your comfort zone. If you can live with them, then stretch away. If not, find something else to stretch you. I'm sure you have plenty of places you can grow. I know I do.

You can start with the things that push your buttons. When you find yourself getting upset, stop and ask why. Consider why you are getting upset in this situation, what you are uncomfortable with. The only reason you get upset is because you made a judgment call about the situation, and you found it lacking in some way. Nothing has meaning except the meaning you give it. So think about what meaning you have given to the situation that causes you discomfort. Let's take traffic as an example, because so many people become upset for no reason. When I was a driver education teacher, I told my students that no one wakes up in the morning and decides to cause a traffic jam to ruin someone's day. Everyone on the road is just trying to get where they want and need to go. They are not waiting around the corner to pull out and cut you off. Like you, they are likely heading to work or home, so cut them some slack and give them a real wave, not the one-fingered one. Smile, wish them well, and mean it. Why get stressed about something as little as that? If traffic really bothers you, leave earlier or later. Stay after work or school until the traffic has cleared, or get up earlier so you can leave before it gets too thick.

My husband drives an eighteen wheeler to provide for us and spends a lot of time on the road every day. He drives thousands of miles each month and, in the process, sees lots of stupid moves by others. People who drive cars, for the most part, have no idea what it takes to drive a truck and trailer that weigh almost eighty thousand pounds. Think back to your physics class and the equation $E=mc^2$. That means that the energy of something is equal to the mass times the speed. Take your speed and multiply it by your weight. For the truck that would be 55 mph x 80,000 lbs = 4,400,000 pounds of force at impact. Slow down and give yourself space to maneuver and don't cut anyone off. Stay calm and don't have distractions. The next time you are on the road and you see a big rig, remember that the driver is just doing the job of carrying stuff to your local store so you can buy it and is not trying to tick you off. Give the driver a wave and a smile, and let the truck in. It's all about perspective and how you see things. If you find yourself getting upset, check in and ask why, see what comes up, and then deal with it in an appropriate way.

You can take a page out of someone else's book as well. Look around at the people who appear to be handling things the way you would like to. There are plenty of good examples to follow. They can give you ideas for what to do and how to handle things you haven't experienced yet. They can be role models for you and help you grow. You can pick the best from everyone and apply it to your life. You will find yourself better equipped to deal with life as it unfolds before you. You'll find you have strengths and abilities you didn't know you had, all because you took the personal challenge laid before you. You took the challenge to grow and to invest in yourself and your family. You'll find it has made all the difference when you are on the porch of your dream home, looking back.

What you have learned from this chapter:

You must stretch your comfort zone now to grow.

You will have change in your life. Use it to make yourself better.

What you want to remember:

9

ASK QUESTIONS

"Take charge of your life by taking charge of your thoughts."
— Jeanie Cisco-Meth

So far we have focused on internal work and understanding bullying. Now we'll get into the action part of bully proofing you. Most bullies are not making decisions or processing information when they are in the act of bullying. They are in survival mode, reacting to the emotions and stress inside of them. What that means, without getting too technical, is that they are in reactionary mode. Some of them are looking for ways to fit in, and they believe they can accomplish this by bringing you down. We spent a good deal of time on this in chapter four, so I just want to touch on it here.

Bullies see their victims as people who can help them reach their goal of feeling better by hurting someone else. If you have applied the lessons learned in the first three chapters, their mean words will not impact you because you have built your personal value. How cool is that? Can I get a big smile? Thanks.

The best way I found for my students to combat bullying was to move the bully into a thinking state. You also have to be in a thinking state. That is why we've done all the work on moving through fear and being able to handle the stress of it. When you are being bullied, you enter a state of fear, and if you haven't learned how to handle fear appropriately, you won't. If you find you have difficulty moving through fear, my coaching/mentoring program can help you.

In chapter seven we discussed why you need to learn how to react appropriately when facing things that frighten you. Now you'll put it to use. You need to be able to think of questions to ask in the moment. I suggest you have some "go-to" questions that you can use in the beginning. For example, "Oh, are you talking to me?" "I didn't know. Can you repeat that, please?" Because people seldom do this, the bully will not expect it and will pause and process what you just said. This is often all that is needed. It is a form of a pattern interrupt that is used in neuro-linguistic programming and that Tony Robbins made popular in his work. Many others now use some form of it to help their clients. You can use it to stop bullying.

Questions have to be answered. You have been asked questions for your entire life and have been expected to answer them. You have been programmed to answer them, and so has everyone around you. What's your favorite color? You probably just answered. You can't help yourself, and neither can the bully. You also had to think about your answer. You were moved from one mode to another in a fraction of a second. Do you like ice cream? Did it again. Sorry, I'll stop now.

In chapter ten we will cover practicing, but you can start now if you want. The next time your friend asks you a question, ask one back. See what happens.

"Can we go to lunch? Will you pay?", asks your friend.

Ask a question back. "Did you paint your bedroom last night?" You can't ask an expected question—that answer is already planned.

"Huh? Did you just ask me if I painted my bedroom?"

"Yes. Did you?" You can go on with this as long as you need. It's fun and they'll forget about asking for you to pay for lunch and you can ask them to pay

Now that you have learned how to use a simple question to make someone pause and start thinking, let's cover how to phrase the questions. You want to ask questions that are unexpected. You want to make the bully think about what you just asked. Let's go over some examples. You just walked out of the lunch room when you are confronted. You ask, "What did you have for lunch today?"

The bully had the hamburger.

"I chose the pizza. Did you like the hamburger?"

Yes or no. It doesn't matter.

"That's cool. Have a good day." You walk away.

You started a conversation with someone who wanted to intimidate you, and it appeared to have no effect on you whatsoever. You just handled a bully in a way that can be admired by others. Celebrate...maybe not right in front of everyone, but in the bathroom or gym. Find a place to let yourself feel good about what just happened. Lock that feeling in so that the next time it happens, your successes back you up.

At our house, we do the Snoopy dance. Snoopy is the black-and-white dog from *Peanuts* that loves to dance. Go rent any show with Charlie Brown in it and watch Snoopy dance to Schroeder's music. It will make you smile. Now picture your entire family doing the Snoopy dance. If Snoopy is not your thing, find something that is.

If you watch sports at all, you see people locking in wins all the time. Tiger Woods does the fist pull. Football players smack each other on the behinds and do chest bumps. It doesn't matter what you do, just do something. The easiest state to change is your physical state. Your physical state changes your mental state.

Sit or stand up straight. Pull your shoulders back. Take a deep breath and blow it out. Put a big smile on your face. You'll feel better. Your physical state changes your mental state. Use that when you're facing fear. Stand in your power. Don't be overpowering, just stand in your power. Stand with your head up, your shoulders back, and a smile on your face, and see how your life changes. If you are feeling down, check your posture. I'll bet you're slumped.

Another place you might encounter a bully could be in the hallway. You are told something unpleasant.

You ask, "What class did you just finish?"

The class doesn't matter.

"Oh. I had math. I love math. How about you?"

Whether the bully hates it or loves it doesn't matter.

"OK. Have a great day."

Whatever class you use, say you loved it. This puts you in a happy mood, and happy is power. You don't have to say the class you were just in. You can say the one you are heading to. Your answer must be true. If you are lying, it will show in your body language and dis-empower you. Be happy, and be strong.

Let's look at another example. This time, someone gets in your face outside, either before or after school.

You ask, "What time did you get here this morning?"

Again, the time doesn't matter.

"Yeah. I got here at seven-thirty. Have a wonderful day."

Again, be honest and always wish the bully a happy day. The exact words don't matter. Just make them positive and uplifting. This will keep you in a position of power without belittling or taking the other person's power away.

The questions above are good starting questions that you can practice and memorize. They will help give you success right from the start. You can come up with your own later. You will always be faced with bullies. People—maybe even a friend—will say things that hurt your feelings or make you feel bad. Your responsibility is to decide how those words will impact you and your life. I suggest that if the person saying the hurtful thing is important to you, explain how it made you feel and why. This can save your friendship and prevent more hurt feelings. Sometimes things are said that bring back painful memories. The other person doesn't know everything about you and your past. Without meaning to, someone might say a word that triggers you. I said something to my daughter the other day when I was trying to be funny. When I saw her face, I knew I had hurt her. It was a mistake and I apologized and asked for her forgiveness. If I had not been paying attention or looking at her when I said it, I might not have known. I believe she would have told me later, but it would have been painful for her until she talked with me about it. Thank goodness I saw my impact immediately and could speak with her and we could understand each other and lessen the pain. There was under-standing and forgiveness within a short period of time. I am grateful for that.

I never want to hurt someone, but sometimes it happens. That might be the case in the situation with your friend. Ask the questions to find out.

Questions are mainly used to gather information. When you ask a question, you show interest in the other person. You are saying that the person's opinion matters to you. People love to feel important and have their ideas, thoughts, feelings, and concerns listened to. That's all everyone is looking for: to feel special. Gather information about people, talk to them about themselves, and you will always have a friend.

Look at each day as a chance to learn and grow, to find new ways to do things, to engage in new experiences, and to meet new people. If you believe that life is a learning experience, you naturally want to learn. You are more likely to be curious about things and not form opinions until you gather more information. That's the approach you'll take for bully proofing yourself.

When approached with a tense situation, you need to stay calm and ask questions rather than just react. Think about what is happening and how best to respond. Ask yourself questions. Do you need to run away because it is potentially life threatening, or can you deflect the bully's attention with a question? Will making a positive statement about yourself take care of the situation? Are there others around you that you need to protect? Would you be happy with your behavior if it showed up on YouTube? What does your reaction say about you? Questions like these need to be answered in the moment but thought out ahead of time. You are more likely to stick to your decisions when you are stressed if you think about them when you are calm and unstressed. That's why it's important to practice and walk through some of these scenarios before you are faced with them.

I don't understand why people practice sports but won't practice other things. Practice the things in life you want to get better at. Practice talking with loved ones about things you find difficult. Practice thinking when faced with fearful situations. If you practice and then measure, monitor, and adjust, you will get better. Practice makes permanent. You have to make it perfect.

Now to recap what you learned:

Create a pattern interrupt with your questions.

Stay honest and positive when facing a bully.

Phrase your questions to change the mood of the situation.

Stay calm.

Look at it as a learning experience.

Celebrate your wins with joy and abandon.

Create a physical move you can use to remind yourself of your win.

Remember you are who you decide to be, and not who the bully says.

Use power statements about yourself in your head. "I got this." "I am beautiful and loved."

Keep it simple.

Remember that you're going to be fine.

What you want to remember:

PRACTICE, PRACTICE, PRACTICE...PERFECTION!

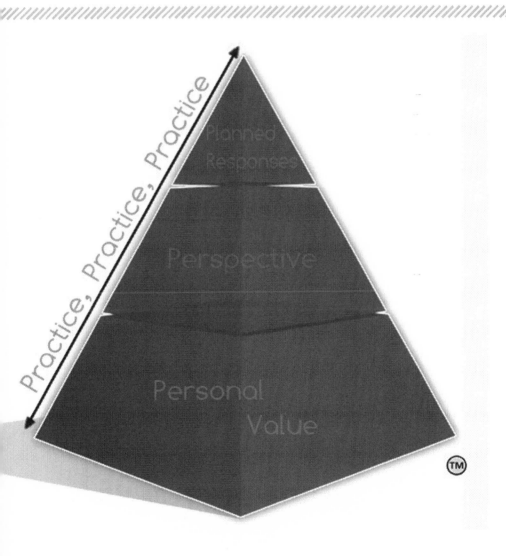

10

PRACTICE, PRACTICE, PRACTICE … PERFECTION!

"Always bear in mind that your own resolution to succeed is more important than any other."
— *Abraham Lincoln*

This chapter holds the second-most important concept for you to master. The first and most important is increasing your confidence and personal value.

I believe practice is the only way to get better at anything. You'll never do something perfectly the first time. However, if you do something new, ask yourself what went right, what went wrong, what you need to change—and then make those changes—you will approach perfection. Practice does not make perfect. It just makes it permanent. You must measure, monitor, and adjust your actions through the results you achieve. If you have what you want, keep doing what you're doing. If you want something different, you must do something new. When you do something new, you will not be proficient at it the first few times. You need to practice.

You will need thought and insight to understand what you want to accomplish. **Create a win-win situation, one in which both you and the bully are left feeling good about yourselves**. Bystanders will also have a great example to follow in the future to help themselves deal with difficult situations as well. The environment in which the bullying took place is still safe for others, and you feel good about yourself.

There are basically two types of practice, mental and physical. In mental practice, also called visualization, you practice only in your mind. Most people do this, but they practice the wrong things. "I have been through some terrible things in my life, some of which actually happened," Mark Twain wrote. Everyone has done this to some degree. Now you need to practice the good experiences. Think about how you want something to unfold, how you would like others to treat you, how you would like your day to progress. You are in control of your thoughts. You can create anything you want. This may be difficult at first because few people practice this skill. The bad things keep popping in. Just say, "Thank you for sharing," and get your mind back on the track you want it on. Harness the incredible power of your mind. Just like anything you practice physically, it takes time, and you will have to measure, monitor, and adjust what you are doing. The first time you tried to walk or talk, it didn't work out well. Now you do both all the time without even thinking about it. You can always look to sports to find people who spend hours every day working on one simple move. They are trying to get just a fraction better. Athletes have been using visualization as part of their practice routines for quite some time now.

When you visualize, your neurons fire and build a pathway. This neural pathway makes it easier for the same action to take place again. The more you travel the pathway in your mind or with your movements, the easier it becomes to travel. So practice what you'll say when you feel uncomfortable or nervous. The more you practice, the easier it becomes, and the more comfortable you are.

The more complex a task is, the more difficult it is to first learn to perform it. Start with simple, and progress in complexity. Take your task and break it into smaller parts. Learn the parts, and then put them together to create a whole. The same is true when you are coming up with questions or comments to use in tough situations.

Let's walk through an example. You and your best friend have been dealing with bullies and are tired of it. You come up with a plan to practice your questions on each other. You spend time on the weekend and in the evenings asking each other the questions. Then you take turns being the bully. When you are the bully, you don't start a verbal attack. Only say, "I am approaching you" or, "I am here" or, "Let's begin." You don't want to practice being a bully. You want to practice only what you want to get better at, and that is dealing with a bully in an appropriate way. Take turns going first and responding. Make sure you are comfortable asking the questions. Now it's time to take it to the next level. You have to get uncomfortable again.

Once you can run through the questions with ease, turn up the heat. Running through them with your friend is not the same as the real thing. You want your practice to be as close to the real thing as possible. Now you're going to practice in public. Pick a place with lots of people where you might be embarrassed. (Remember, you'll take this step after you have worked on pushing the boundaries of your comfort zone. You should have experience with pushing through fear at this point. If you don't, go back to chapter 8 and do it.) One of you will go first. Walk toward each other, and the person playing the bully will say, "Let's begin" or one of the other statements you have practiced. Ask your questions, and then walk away. In my live trainings, we do this right in the training. It greases the wheels and gets you going. You'll get nervous and might forget the question, or you might stumble through. Do it again and again and again. Practice until the fear is gone and you can move smoothly through the scenario.

Now move your practice to the place where the bullying occurred. This will, once again, raise the anxiety level. Practice the questions and answers just as you have been. Continue working with the person you started this exercise with. Practice the questions and answers until you are comfortable with them.

Now you are ready to ask the bully the questions you have so faithfully practiced. You are ready to deal with the bully in an appropriate way. You can be an example to those around you on how to control your reactions.

When you follow these steps, they become habits. When they become habits, you don't have to think about them anymore. When you don't have to think about them anymore, you have bully proofed yourself. You will be ready for anyone who might try to bully you. You are bully proofed for life.

You will have a deeper understanding of yourself and others. You will have a deeper understanding of life and how precious it is. You will have a deeper understanding of how important friends are.

When you are practicing, remember you will get better as you measure, monitor, and adjust to get the results you want.

The steps to follow:

1. Find others to work with.
2. Tell them what is happening.
3. Come up with the questions to ask.
4. Set up how you will celebrate.
5. Define the practice scenario.
6. Make sure the environment is safe.
7. Have safety words you can use if you need a break.
8. Take turns asking the questions and responding.
9. Move the practice to a public place once you are comfortable.
10. Move the practice to the place the bullying occurs once you are comfortable.
11. Practice until you feel you are ready.
12. Remember, you can do this. I know you can.
13. Celebrate and reward yourself along the way.

Don't get discouraged. Just keep working on it until you are proficient. You have learned to do other things, and you can learn this as well. You can do this and be bully proof for life, or you can shrink back in fear.

You don't have to do any of the things I'm telling you, but if you want a change, you must take action. Right now. Today. Start small and build up. You don't need a time factor but a belief and practice factor. It will take as long as it takes, but the sooner you start, the sooner you will be living your life and controlling your reactions to it.

What you learned:

Practice in a safe environment.

Reward yourself for taking the steps needed to bully proof yourself.

Measure, monitor, and adjust to get the results you desire.

Expect the first practice run to be different from the tenth one.

Stand in your power and live your life.

What you want to remember:

11

//

WHAT NOW?

"The future is not something you enter. It is created by your actions."
— *Jeanie Cisco-Meth*

As you follow the steps laid out in this book, you'll find your life has changed for the better. You'll have more confidence. You'll be more secure and understanding in your dealings with others. You'll be better equipped to deal with life's challenges. Some of you may be a little bit afraid of what will happen now. Will it really work? You might be afraid of a physical attack. I understand your fear and I know you can move through it.

I know that if you follow the steps laid out here, you will lessen the impact others have on you. You truly will be bully proof. I can say that because I have taught the process to others and it has worked time and time again. No one I know followed these steps and had bullying escalate. It has never progressed past the verbal stage.

My theory for this is that bullying is addictive for some. They feel powerful and important. With any drug, the effects get weaker and you need to increase the dosage to get the same effect. I believe that is why verbal attacks can lead to physical attacks. The offender needs to up the offence to get the same benefits, the same rush. I have never heard of a bully attacking a new target physically the first time they began bullying. Bullying always starts with a verbal attack, and then progresses to physical attacks. If you stop it in the first stage, you don't have to worry about the second stage.

If you are ever attacked physically, you must report it and get help immediately. There are support groups everywhere, in your school, your community, your home, your friend's home, the police station, or grocery store. You just need to tell someone. If you don't, it will get worse. The abuse will continue to escalate until it is stopped.

If you witness someone else being bullied, you can help by following the steps outlined in the ask questions chapter. You can ask, "Excuse me. Can you tell me where classroom 216 is?" Approach bullies as though you have no idea they are verbally attacking someone. Try to deflect their attention and get them thinking again. Get them off their power surge/fix. If you witness a physical attack, call an adult or 911, depending on who is involved. Everyone has cell phones now and no one will know who reported it. Many schools and work places have phone numbers you can call to report bullying or harassment anonymously.

You can stop bullying. You have the power to make a difference in your life and in the lives of others. Apply the lessons you have learned in this book. Trust them to do what I have told you they will do, and then teach them to others.

CONCLUSION

Thank you

Thank you for your time and dedication to making society a safer place for all. Your ability to deal with bullying in a safe and appropriate way will help yourself and others. You can be the change you wish to see in the world by starting today. It takes courage to stand up and make a difference. It takes strength to make changes. It takes intelligence to see and understand why you are doing something.

Thank you for being courageous, strong, and intelligent. You are a leader in your community. Thank you for making a difference.

See you soon,
Jeanie Cisco-Meth
Author, Trainer, Mentor

APPENDIX A

SOME OF THE GREAT BOOKS I HAVE READ

The Art of Significance by Dan Clark

Little Voice Mastery by Blair Singer

Leadership by Stephen R. Cover

Awaken the Giant Within by Anthony Robbins

The Science of Success by Wallace D. Wattles

Life Without Limits by Nick Vujicic

Born to Win by Zig Ziglar

Influencer by Patterson, Grenny, Maxfield, McMillan, and Switzler

Millionaire Dropouts by Woody Woodward

The Power of Intention by Dr. Wayne W. Dyer

Unstoppable by Cynthia Kersey

The Pursuit of Happyness by Chris Gardner

Lincoln on Leadership by Donald T. Phillips

The Time of My Life by Patrick Swayze

Always Looking Up by Michael J. Fox

Three Feet from Gold by Lechter and Reid

Driven by Larry H. Miller

Get Motivated by Tamara Lowe

No Limits by Michael Phelps

Worth Fighting For by Lisa Niemi Swayze

Start Where You Are by Chris Gardner

Crucial Conversations by Patterson, Grenny, McMillan, and Switzler

My Story by Elizabeth Smart

Still Me by Christopher Reeve

Success Through a Positive Mental Attitude by Napoleon Hill and Clement Stone

Change Anything by Patterson, Grenny, Maxfield, McMillan, and Switzler

Harmonic Wealth by James Arthur Ray

Love Your Life by Victoria Osteen

The Winning Spirit by Joe Montana

My Stroke of Insight by Jill Bolte Taylor, PhD

The Story of My Life by Helen Keller

My Unbelievably True Life Story by Arnold Schwarzenegger

Tuesdays with Morrie by Mitch Albom

The Dalai Lama: His Essential Wisdom edited by Carol Kelly-Gangi

Live What You Love by Bob and Melinda Blanchard

Seabiscuit by Laura Hillenbrand

Become a Better You by Joel Osteen

When God Winks at You by Squire Rushmell

Everything Happens for a Reason by Mira Kirshenbaum

Catch Fire: How to Ignite Your Own Economy by Douglas Scott Nelson

The Butterfly Effect by Andy Andrews

Secrets of the Millionaire Mind T. Harv Eker

The Four Spiritual Laws of Prosperity by Edwene Gaines

The Holy Bible

The Ultimate Gift by Jim Stovall

Any of the books published by Simple Truths

Appendix B

SOME GREAT MOVIES I HAVE SEEN

The Ultimate Gift, 20th Century Fox, 2007

Field of Dreams, Universal Pictures, 1989

Les Misérables, Columbia Pictures and Mandalay Entertainment, 1998

The Sound of Music, 20th Century Fox, 1965

It's a Wonderful Life, Republic Pictures, 1947

Seabiscuit, DreamWorks Pictures and Universal Studios, 2003Radio

Rudy, Tri Star, 2000

Take the Lead, New Line Home Entertainment, Inc., 2006

Coach Carter, Paramount and MTV, 2005The Blind Side

Brian's Song, Columbia Pictures, 1971

The Blind Side, Warner Brothers Entertainment, 2009

Amazing Grace, 20th Century Fox, 2007

Radio, Columbia Pictures and Revolution Studios, 2004

Shallow Hal, 20th Century Fox, 2001

Freedom Writers, Paramount and MTV, 2007

Forever Strong, Picture Rock Entertainment and Crane Movie Co., 2009

Rocky Series, Metro Goldwyn Mayer and 20th Century Fox, 1975-2006

Glory Road, Walt Disney, 2006

Gridiron Gang, Columbia Pictures, 2006

Hoosiers, Metro Goldwyn Mayer and 20th Century Fox, 1986

Invincible, Walt Disney, 2006

ABOUT THE AUTHOR

Jeanie Cisco-Meth was born Avis Marjean Cisco. Martha, Jeanie's mother, wanted to name her after her own mother who had died when Martha was only nine. Jeanie's father, Delbert, wanted to call her Jeanie. They reached a compromise and she was called Jeanie but named Avis. This led to some confusion when Jeanie's mother enrolled her in Lewis County Adventist Academy in Chehalis, Washington.

Martha said, "I am here to register Avis Cisco for school."

Jeanie replied, "My name is Jeanie."

Martha said, "Your real name is Avis, but you are called Jeanie."

Jeanie said, "Really? OK."

She was born in Twin Falls, Idaho, but was raised on a dairy farm in Morton, Washington. She spent almost every day riding her pony, Dusty, and later her horse, Sugar. She has many fond memories of the farm and feels blessed to have been raised there. She says, "I believe that the farm helped make me who I am today. It gave me responsibility at an early age and taught me to care for life."

She talks about bringing every stray home she could get a rope on.

"Look, Dad, it followed me home."

"Why is there a rope on it?"

"I don't know."

Animals where her true friends. She spent many hours with them because, "They never yelled at me or put me down. They just loved me. They couldn't read or write either." Jeanie had many learning disabilities growing up and struggled in school. She was told by teachers she would never make it past high school and would be lucky to make it there. She remembers how hard it was just to get passing grades. "I felt like just giving up many times then someone would tell me I was stupid or laugh when I tried to read and it would tick me off. I became determined to make it just to prove everyone wrong."

She also enjoyed basketball and remembers talking with Coach's wife on a trip back home from college.

"I remember the day you showed up at school," Coach's wife said. "My husband came home so excited. He said, 'We have a tall one.' He could hardly wait for basketball to start."

Morton Jr.-Sr. High had three hundred enrolled students in grades seven through twelve. Jeanie's graduating class was twenty-five students in the spring of 1985.

Jeanie remembers tryouts a little differently. Even though she loved basketball, she had never played organized ball. It was a big change for her. She had never had a coach. Before making the Morton basketball team she figured it out the best she could by watching others. She says, "Coach used to tell me, 'Jump higher. I can't even slip my clipboard under your feet.' It was real nice to hear Coach was excited for me to play. It was his belief in me that helped me become a better player. I went from riding the pine for junior varsity in my junior year to starting varsity as a senior. Coach and I spent a lot of time in the gym that summer and it all paid off."

She used the same tenacity to make the team she used to make it through classes. During basketball she found her strength. She learned she could push her body to do things to get positive recognition. She could lift more weight and do more push-ups than most.

When she was in the Military, she did 1000 push-ups a day so she could max the men's physical fitness test. "I never felt it was right to have different standards for women as for men. We were expected to do the same jobs so we should have the same standards." A perfect score on the physical fitness was 300. Her highest score was 297. The run was always the most difficult. Military personal are required to test periodically during their training. The physical fitness test is two minutes of push-ups, two minutes of sit-ups, and a two mile run. "I could do 97 sit-ups, 92 push-ups, and the run in 11:58. I always missed points on the run."

She found joy in accomplishing hard things. "It was easier for me to push my body than my mind. I struggled so much and took verbal abuse from so many because my brain didn't work the way everyone else's did. I got tired of being the outsider so I found something I was good at and excelled at it."

"The thought of writing a book scared the crap out of me. It took a while for others to convince me I had to do it. I did it because I want to help others. I want to heal others from their pain and a book can help me do that. It can reach more people than I can. It can be read again and again and given to friends and family. That is my wish, to start a ripple that spreads through homes, communities, states, countries, and the world. I want others to build themselves up so they can still stand when discouraging things are said to them. I want to help you build your confidence and personal value. Thank you for listening."

Jeanie understands the value of hard work and determination. It is what brought her to where she is today. She knows more of the same will propel her toward her new dreams.

She married Laurence Meth on October 13, 2002, and says it was one of the best decisions she ever made. They reside in Cedar Hills, Utah. They still have two kids at home, as well as a dog and a cat. They also have a son who lives in Colorado and one who lives in Roy, Utah.

Is your
"Little Voice"
beating you up?

Telling you things like you are not good
enough, smart enough, successful
enough...enough of anything!

STOP THE
BEATING NOW!

Go to www.BlairSinger.com now and take the
FREE Little Voice Diagnostic Test.
Find out if your Little Voice is helping or hurting you.

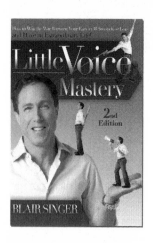

With *Little Voice Mastery*, you will learn to:

Maintain your power in any situation

Stop the debilitating chatter so you
can attract what you want

End procrastination and resurrect
level 10 confidence in any situation

Break through self-sabotaging habits

...in 30 seconds or less so you can
eliminate hidden blockages and
experience floods of income!

Resources include the *Little Voice Mastery* book and CD. You can
buy them both at a special package rate at www.BlairSinger.com

PEAK POTENTIALS™

www.peakpotentials.com

T. Harv Eker is author of the #1 NY Times bestselling book, Secrets of the Millionaire Mind, and his programs have really helped me, as well as hundreds of thousands of people all over the world.

In his book, Harv teaches you how to identify your "financial blueprint" which is our ability to be successful. Unfortunately, as I quickly learned, many of us have an extremely low blueprint. But--and this is big--you can learn to RESET your blueprint for a higher level of success.

Do you remember the first time you tried riding a bike? It was hard, but after lots of practice and maybe a bit of falling down, you suddenly found your balance and began riding with ease. Well, that feeling of suddenly being able to ride is exactly how I feel about my life since attending Harv's program, the Millionaire Mind Intensive.

They'll teach you all about:
* The hidden cause of almost all financial problems
* How your childhood is affecting you financially today
* How to RESET your financial thermostat for automatic success
* How to train your "mind" to work for you, instead of against you
There are events scheduled in cities all across the US and Canada. They're even offering free General Seating registration!

Get the most recent list of upcoming events and register now:

http://www.peakambassador.com/cmd.php?af=mmi27652&p=15

I hope you take advantage of this rare and amazing opportunity to transform your entire life--I did, and I'm glad!

Sincerely,

Jeanie Cisco-Meth

JeanieCisco·Meth

I want to give you a gift for reading and incorporating what you have learned into your life. Please go to my website www.jeanieciscometh.com or www.bullyproofingyou.com, send me an email, and you will receive 15% off of any regular priced item.

If you would like to teach this program to others, please send me an email explaining your ideas. I would love to work with you in spreading this powerful and much needed message.

When you are at one of my live events, please come talk to me. I would love to get to know you better.

Until we meet again,

Jeanie Cisco-Meth

Leta Greene's *How To Embrace Your Inner Hotness*

You'll learn:

- To transform the way you see and present yourself, inside and out
- That "different" isn't bad it's the key to hotness
- How to choose happiness now, no matter your current situation
- How to stop letting other people define your worth, potential, and purpose

Buy your copy today at http://letagreene.com/book or on Amazon.com

94650932R00102

Made in the USA
Columbia, SC
04 May 2018